Postdigital Ethical Futures

Postdigital Ethical Futures emerged from the work of the Ethical Futures Network hosted by the William Temple Foundation meeting both online and at Trinity College, Oxford. This book illustrates the research being carried out by some of the members of this network by examining the more practical aspects of the subject of religion and the digital, drawing on a wider range of disciplines and was created in memory of John Reader whose idea the text was, who died suddenly in 2023. This book examines issues of ethics as encountered in both the digital and environmental spheres, and seeks to cross the boundary between philosophy and theology.

Maggi Savin-Baden is a Professor and Senior Research Fellow at Blackfriars Hall, University of Oxford. She has authored, coauthored and edited 27 books in the areas of innovative learning, digital fluency, digital afterlife pedagogical agents, qualitative research methods, problem-based learning and the metaverse. She is currently a co-editor of the *Metaverse* book series. In her spare time, she runs, bakes, climbs, does triathlons and wild swimming.

Maria Power is a Senior Research Fellow at the Las Casas Institute for Social Justice, Blackfriars Hall, University of Oxford. Her work focuses mainly on peace-building within divided communities in Northern Ireland. Her most recent publications include *Catholic Social Teaching and Theologies of Peace in Northern Ireland: Cardinal Cahal Daly and the Pursuit of the Peaceable Kingdom* (Routledge, 2021) and *Violence and Peace in Sacred Texts* (2023). She is currently writing a monograph exploring the role of the bible in the conflict in Northern Ireland which will be published by Routledge in 2025.

Postdigital Ethical Futures

Essays in Honour of John Reader

Edited by: Maggi Savin-Baden
and Maria Power

CRC Press
Taylor & Francis Group
Boca Raton London New York

CRC Press is an imprint of the
Taylor & Francis Group, an **informa** business
A CHAPMAN & HALL BOOK

Designed cover image: Shutterstock_2540223667

First edition published 2026
by CRC Press
2385 NW Executive Center Drive, Suite 320, Boca Raton FL 33431

and by CRC Press
4 Park Square, Milton Park, Abingdon, Oxon, OX14 4RN

CRC Press is an imprint of Taylor & Francis Group, LLC

ISBN: 978-1-032-80654-9 (hbk)
ISBN: 978-1-032-80580-1 (pbk)
ISBN: 978-1-003-49795-0 (ebk)

DOI: 10.1201/9781003497950

Typeset in Times
by codeMantra

For our friend John Reader

Contents

PART III Theoretical Debates

PART IV Endings

Contributors

Andrew Bevan is a Baptist minister who worked in accountancy, the NHS, and a Christian drug and alcohol rehabilitation charity, before training for ordination in Oxford where he is now based. He is keen to develop his understanding, and a conceptual framework which is adequate for the unprecedented challenges from technology and environmental change to help congregations live out their faith in the contemporary world.

Mark Coeckelbergh is a Professor of Philosophy of Media and Technology at the University of Vienna and author of *AI Ethics*, *The Political Philosophy of AI* and *Why AI Undermines Democracy.*

Nuraan Davids is a Professor of Philosophy of Education and the Chair of the Department of Education Policy Studies in the Faculty of Education at Stellenbosch University. Her research interests include philosophy of (higher) education; democratic citizenship education and Islamic philosophy of education. Her most recent books include *Academic Citizenship, Identity, Knowledge, and Vulnerability*; *Out of Place: An Autoethnography of Postcolonial Citizenship.*

Adrian Evans is an Associate Professor at the Centre for Agroecology, Water and Resilience, Coventry University. He leads the 'Policies and Governance for Resilient Food and Water Systems' research cluster. Adrian's research focuses on socio-economic and ethical issues related to agri-food and environmental systems. Adrian is interested in ethical theories that ground ethics in everyday lived experiences.

Peter Haslehurst is a neuroscientist with an interest in machine learning and neural networks. He spent 28 years in the IT industry working as a technical software specialist. In 2007, he enrolled at KCL for a Masters in Neuroscience, followed by a PhD at UCL. Between 2012 and his retirement in 2021, he worked at the Emptage group at Oxford, using novel optical imaging techniques to investigate plasticity at individual synapses. He is a lifelong board games enthusiast.

Aline Knapp is a research associate in Practical Theology at the University of Bonn and at the URPP 'Digital Religion(s)' at the University of Zurich. Her current research focuses on postdigital spirituality, specifically analysing the use of a religious app. In addition to her work on digital theology, she is interested in queer and feminist theology.

Sabrina Müller is the Chair of Practical Theology at the University of Bonn, Germany, and a project leader of the URPP 'Digital Religion(s)' at the University of Zurich. She co-chairs the AAR's Practical Theology Unit and serves on the boards of both IAPT and ISERT. Her work encompasses digital, postcolonial, and feminist practical theologies, as well as church innovation. She is the author of six monographs and has published widely in leading academic journals.

John Reader has degrees from Oxford (MA), Manchester (MPhil) and a PhD from the University of Wales, Bangor. A retired parish priest of over 40 years in ministry, he was also a senior research fellow of the William Temple Foundation; honorary senior lecturer in the School of Education, University of Worcester and senior tutor for the Christian Rural and Environmental Studies course based at Ripon College Cuddesdon. He has published six solo books and co-written a further six. He was instrumental in curating the Ethical Futures Network which has met at Trinity College, Oxford. John died on Sunday, 1 October 2023 after a short illness, and is very much missed.

Simon Reader is the author of *The Ethics of Choosing Children*, part of the book series *Palgrave Studies in Ethics and Public Policy*. He has held positions at Lancaster and Keele University, where he lives with his husband and two young sons.

Eric Trozzo is a Lutheran pastor and theologian currently serving a congregation in New Jersey. He is an honorary research associate at Australian Lutheran College, University of Divinity, Adelaide, Australia and adjunct faculty at Trinity Lutheran Seminary, Capital University, Columbus, OH, USA. He has taught at numerous seminaries internationally.

Paul Woods is an outward-facing theological educator at large with OMF International, UK. He is a non-resident faculty member at Singapore Bible College's School of Advanced Studies and doctoral research mentor for the Asia Graduate School of Theology (Alliance), based in Malaysia. Apart from artificial intelligence, his principal research interests are ecotheology and contextual theology.

Foreword

It's a huge honour to write the foreword to this fascinating collection of essays, co-edited by Professor Maggi Savin-Baden and my late father, Revd Dr John Reader.

When Maggi approached me with the invitation to write something, she explained that the authors saw it as a kind of festschrift to my father, and so I'd like to take this opportunity to say a little about him. It seems appropriate to describe it as a kind of festschrift, for he was what you might call a kind of academic; he was a scholar of course, but he combined this with his life and work as a rural Anglican parish priest in a way that was rare and distinctive.

One of his great gifts was for initiating and sustaining networks of colleagues and friends, often giving rise to unique publications like this one. An alternative Latin term for festschrift is *liber amicorum*, or book of friends, and I think this is how he would have seen this volume. An affinity of experts, academics and inquisitors from different walks of life, all with something new and interesting to say on his latest favourite topic. Nothing captured this better than the Ethical Futures Network, showcased in this collection, which was formally hosted by the William Temple Foundation but behind which my father was a driving force.

Dad's interest in the digital, postdigital, AI and emerging technologies was a little surprising to those of us familiar with his day-to-day encounters with modern conveniences. He was a little intimidated by the internet when it first became part of our lives, but once he realised what a tool emails could be for networking and communicating you would scarcely see him without his battered old Blackberry bulging in his breast pocket. He would simultaneously (and often instantaneously) field enquiries from professors, publishers and, most importantly, his parishioners. Dad passed away suddenly, just a few months after coming out of retirement to become a parish priest again; ministry was in his blood, and a life apart from holy orders didn't suit him in the end.

Others have paid tribute to his rare ability to move between the two worlds of the parish and academia effortlessly and authentically; of how he walked through his parishes not with heavy tomes under his arm, but with a smile on his face, a kind word and willingness to engage with everyone. Some weeks after he died, a story hitherto unknown to anyone reached us from one of his old parishes about someone who professed that Dad had saved her life. Fielding phone calls in the vicarage as a teenager I used to tease him about being his parishioners' fourth emergency service, but I suppose sometimes he really was.

In his dialogue with Mark Coeckelbergh (Chapter 2), there is a section called Crossing Boundaries, where Dad describes his own position as both a priest/practitioner and an academic. He got his hands dirty on the front line of faith and ministry, and brought the fingerprints of that work to bear on the theory. Equally, he took complex and novel theoretical ideas and was able to communicate them with clarity and subtlety to new and different audiences. In his ministry, Dad traversed boundaries across faith and non-faith communities to address shared commitments to issues such as the environment, education and housing. In his intellectual life, he crossed boundaries across various academic disciplines to try and get at the truth. He really followed his nose into any subject, regardless of disciplinary thresholds; reading and writing in a free-wheeling and prodigious way across philosophy, theology, sociology, psychology and pretty much everything else.

From Crossing Boundaries, the conversation with Coeckelbergh turns to a final section entitled The Time of Breathing, in which Dad references his love for jazz and, in particular, Miles Davis. It was strange to read his reference to the album 'Kind of Blue', for this was among the music that we played to him in his final days, in late September 2023. All we had left with him at that point was a time of breathing. Breathing that quickened as the chaplain prayed over him, and calmed as my Mum, Christine, read him poetry. She never left his side, and I know he would also want her to be recognised in this foreword, as in all his publications.

Part of the light that goes out, when you lose somebody, is that no one is left to interpret the world quite like that person did. The world seems poorer for not being seen through their eyes. It's hard to think that our own misadventures, interests and experiences will no longer perhaps be woven into one of Dad's sermons or books, as they sometimes were. Six months after he died, our family WhatsApp group abruptly announced 'Dad left', and I'm certain he would have made a sermon out of that. The loss of Dad's perspective on things, his humour, mischief, enjoyment and curiosity are felt keenly by all who knew him.

Dad has now crossed another, final, boundary, and time carries on for those left behind. We're grateful that in this time his friends and colleagues have pressed on with work he had begun, and work that he found so much joy in helping to generate. He would have been very pleased and very proud to see the publication of this collection, this kind of festschrift to a one-of-a-kind priest, teacher and scholar.

Dr Simon Reader, December 2024.

Acknowledgements

This book has been a challenge to create in a changing higher education system and postdigital world.

Our sincerest thanks to Randi Slack at CRC/Taylor and Francis for being so positive when we suggested the idea of this text. Any mistakes and errors are ours.

True peace is not merely the absence of tension; it is the presence of justice.

Martin Luther King, Jr

Introduction

In 2022, Maggi and John Reader co-edited *Postdigital Theologies* which gathered a series of contributions looking explicitly at different areas of Christian doctrine in the light of recent developments in the postdigital. This book emerged from the work of the Ethical Futures Network hosted by the William Temple Foundation meeting both online and at Trinity College, Oxford. This new book will showcase the research being carried out by some of the members of this network by examining the more practical aspects of the subject of religion and the digital, drawing on a wider range of disciplines and was created in memory of John whose idea the text was, who died suddenly in 2023. Mara Power kindly agreed to join me in bringing this collection together. This book is in three parts.

PART I: THE NATURE OF ETHICS

The first part discusses the nature of ethics itself, as it has been pursued in the work of the Ethical Futures Network. The opening chapter is a development of the Ethical Futures Temple Tract *Ethics after New Materialism* (2019) co-written by Evans and Reader using a case study to illustrate the contours and advantages of this approach. It is followed by the online interview/dialogue between Mark Coeckelbergh and John Reader which took place during April 2023 and was published by the Postdigital Science and Education network the following month. This goes deeply into issues of ethics as encountered in both the digital and environmental spheres, and is an original crossing of the boundary between philosophy and theology in line with the modest ethics approach, discussed in Chapter 1.

PART II: PRACTICAL THEOLOGY AND ETHICS

This part contains material of a more practical nature not only addressing issues of sin and prayer from a practical theology perspective but also drawing on philosophical understandings of transhumanism as relevant to the digital. A chapter on digital church reflects on the complexity of these engagements as they are developing, and reaches beyond the obvious institutional dimensions.

PART III: THEORETICAL DEBATES

The final part returns to more theoretical debates and draws on the contested concept of the Commons as it relates to a biblical example, and also to recent research into neuroscience and how new interpretations might be required by this. The current debates about the ethical and spiritual implications of Facial Recognition Technology draw this book to a close and propose new resources, both theological and philosophical, which contribute to this debate.

ENDINGS

The final section of this book closes with John's final chapter on Digital Spirituality and a reflection by Maria on the text as a whole.

This text has been both a privilege and a work of sorrow. We hope it does justice to John, his work, enthusiasm and for always spurring us on.

Maggi and Maria
May 2025

Part I

The Nature of Ethics

1 The Landscape of Postdigital Ethics

Maggi Savin-Baden

INTRODUCTION

Invariably ethics is seen as an activity relating largely to the efficacy of research studies in the context of higher education, grant awarding bodies and a general view about what counts as right and wrong in society. Yet ethics, particularly postdigital ethics, transcends every aspect of society, politics, higher education and religion, from virtual humans to plagiarism, manufacturing self-driving cars and large language models. This chapter begins by reviewing and reflecting on the landscape of postdigital ethics in the 21st century. It then suggests practical responses to ethical concerns and explores ways of dealing with possible (un)ethical technologies.

WHAT IS MEANT BY THE POSTDIGITAL?

The idea of the postdigital is that it is not temporal, it is not 'after' digital; rather it is a critical inquiry into the state of the digital world. The postdigital then is not about positions or spaces inhabited just for a time; it is essentially ungraspable, which relates to the way in which structures, political systems, cultures, languages and technologies differ and change each other and the state of the world. The postdigital then is a stance towards the digital which seeks to challenge the educational, economic and ethical impact of digital technology on humanity and the environment. As a result it is important to the consideration of ethics because it introduces critical debate about the impact of the digital in terms of the economic impact of algorithms and ethical questions such as the use of iSlaves and surveillance undermining privacy. To say that ethics in the postdigital age is complicated is an understatement. Ethics involves such complex logistics because of what is always hidden beneath what we see on the surface of things. Some years ago I was critical of Actor Network Theory (ANT) because of its use in the context of qualitative research approaches where it was adopted with the hallmarks of post-positivism, as exemplified in the seminal post-positivist work of Popper (Popper, 1959). My stance was a challenge to those who argue that ANT is qualitative, invariably because they were using this approach, yet neither documented how they collected data, nor how they analysed data using this approach. However, rereading ANT having realised Latour was from a wine-growing family helped me to see and understand it and

DOI: 10.1201/9781003497950-2

in particular see its relevance to postdigital ethics. Wine growing involves a consideration of everything from soil and grape variety to bottling and corkage. Such processes are actors who contribute to the final outcome. Any disruption affects the wine. In ANT, Latour's focus is to concentrate on the footprints of the actors and examine how each has an impact on the other, in order to construct or see a multidimensional reality (Latour, 1987).

THE LANDSCAPE OF POSTDIGITAL ETHICS

Postdigital ethical futures are the focus of this text, and this chapter examines the landscape of postdigital ethics in order to locate the chapters in the current context of ethics in the 21st century. The argument across the chapters is that postdigital ethics is not straightforward or immutable. In previous generations, there was an assumption that ethical positions provided clear boundaries, guidance, rules and even a form of morality. Yet ethics is not something that is infallible, not once and for all; and in our postdigital world it has become increasingly liminal. What it means to be an ethical human being has become a complex and somewhat troublesome question. Postdigital ethics then is not about prescription before action but is instead an emergent porous and ongoing series of ethical decisions and practices. Central to this is the management of quality of relationships, a commitment to truth, trust and justice and includes an exploration of areas such as applied ethics, theology, the postdigital and what it means to be human.

Postdigital ethics then not only brings together traditional ethical theories, as defined in Table 1.1, but also introduces newer stances towards ethics such as modest ethics. Table 1.1 delineates eight different ethical approaches, outlines the possible stance towards the postdigital and suggests probable practical challenges. Through this table, it is suggested that there are difficulties with some of the more traditional ethical stances. However, it is argued here that modest ethics offer the most realistic and unproblematic means of aligning ethics in the context of the challenges of a postdigital age. The argument here is that postdigital ethics transcends earlier ethical theories and instead combines modest ethics and virtue ethics in a way that seeks to examine truths in ways that are pragmatic and explore moral problems in context. Central to understanding postdigital ethics in this way is a consideration of what it means to be human, which is discussed in the later sections of this chapter.

MODEST ETHICS

It is clear from Table 1.1 that postdigital ethics does not subscribe just to one ethical theory, but as John Reader and I suggest

> Ethics, along with both science and religion, need to exercise a degree of modesty. Claims to establish truth in some exclusive manner, and therefore at the cost of an open engagement with other contributions, need to be tempered by the recognition that no one approach has the monopoly of truth.
>
> *(Reader & Savin-Baden, 2020, p. 300)*

TABLE 1.1
Ethical theories

Form of ethics	Definition	Key characteristics	Perspectives on the postdigital	Practical challenges
Deontological	The focus is on the rightness or wrongness of the actions themselves rather than the consequences	Focus on duty and obligation	Difficult concept to accept as it does not deal with right and wrong	Difficulty in accepting the idea of postdigital ethics when there is an assumption that there are clear boundaries
Utilitarian	The assumption that ethics can be governed by deciding what is right and what is wrong	Belief in the greatest good for humanity	It is a troublesome concept as it has few boundaries	Notion of outcomes and what counts as best is complex in the postdigital realm
Feminist	The belief that traditional ethical standpoints have theorising that has undervalued women's moral experience	Stance towards female empowerment and against oppression	It can help to challenge toxic misogyny	Gender-based oppression in postdigital spaces is hard to counter
Marxist	This is based on the idea that morality is a historical product, and people are conditioned by this	Stance against elite power and economic exploitation	It is seen as interrupting elite narratives and surveillance practices	Surveillance capitalism is largely ignored globally
Situational	The situation itself should be evaluated ethically rather than judging by predefined moral standards	Rejection of prescriptive rules and decisions	Values it because the focus is on context rather than judgement	Circumstances difficult to judge and forgiveness often challenging
Discourse	Ethics and norms are created through discourse	Valuing discourse as a means of reaching understanding and agreement	Believes discourse can help understanding of postdigital ethics	Discourse across cultures poses challenges in postdigital ethics
Virtue ethics	Virtue ethics treat the concept of moral virtue as central to ethics	Actions are those that embody virtuous character traits, such as courage, loyalty or wisdom	Acting virtuously in digital spaces by practising inclusive engagement, self-control and discretion	The assumption that a virtuous person is able to determine and reason what counts as right action
Modest ethics	Modest ethics affirms what a body can do, with what degrees of power, movement or rest	Facing what we cannot control Enhancing life	Seeing the digital as offering possibilities for life enhancement Recognising power in digital spaces	The hope to counter the speed of the digital The optimism of being able to disrupt established binaries of human and non-human

The idea of modest ethics can be aligned with the idea of the postdigital (e.g., Jandrić et al., 2018), since both prompt a rupture in our existing theories. The modest ethics approach rejects over-arching ethical frameworks, their limited respect for the empirical complexities of real-world scenarios and the power and agency that such frameworks ascribe to human rationality. Modest ethics instead embraces a deep interconnection between ethics and materiality, leading to a new kind of worldly ethics, which is more than human in its scope. In practice modest ethics is needed in:

- truth claims
- recognising the impact we have on the environment
- the day-to-day realities of our lives and the ways in which we affect others on whom we depend
- realising the need to reduce and remove convenient practices that are unethical and
- appreciating the power plays in digital spaces.

There is a tendency to construct ethical frameworks in order to cope with such complexity and produce criteria by which we can evaluate human action and make decisions about the right way forward. Modest ethics encourages us to become more comfortable with that which we cannot control and which is constantly moving beyond us. Modest ethics may demand that we move more slowly and carefully, rather than dashing ahead in ways that our culture and digital technology encourage us to do.

Reader and Evans suggest that modest ethics includes the ethics of information and the ethics of digital techno-cultures and are modest with regards to:

- their rejection of over-arching ethical frameworks and their respect for the empirical complexities of real-world scenarios
- the amount of power and agency that they ascribe to human rationality
- their focus on the deep interconnections between ethics and materiality.

(Reader & Evans, 2019, p. 27)

Recovering a language of virtue and modesty will also help us to deal with issues such as dupery, deception and fake news. However, in the postdigital age issues of dupery, deception, fake news and misplaced understandings of algorithms introduce new complexities into ethical debates and concerns.

DUPERY, DECEPTION, FAKE NEWS AND ALGORITHMIC IMAGININGS

The idea of dupery implies that we are tricked in some way, hoodwinked in ways that make us feel the mistake is ours and that we are rather stupid in being so easily taken in. In the 21st century the most common form of acceptable dupery and deception is that of magic, largely because we know we are being deceived and we are fascinated by it.

Dupery

In Shakespeare's plays dupery can be accidental, as in *The Comedy of Errors* (Shakespeare, 1594), which tells the story of two sets of identical twins who were accidentally separated at birth, or drug-induced dreams in *A Midsummer Night's Dream* (Shakespeare, 1605). Sinclair explains that what is central to dupery is the use of emotion to deceive, which occurs through manipulation, distraction and even laughter (Sinclair, 2021). Sinclair (2021) explains that different types of duperies can have different effects and that the common tactics used to manipulate us are misdirection and distraction. She cites a poignant example of where deception was added to a simulation resulting in the death of a mannequin where a senior clinician entered the simulation and asked for the wrong medication to be given. A clear case of planned misdirection. Calhoun et al. describe what occurred in this simulation and argue that there may have been concerns about the stress that such dupery has on students (Calhoun et al., 2015). What such practices do indicate is the need to ensure students are properly debriefed after such deception, something that is also argued for and undertaken in psychology experiments where students are deceived. Whilst the instances she describes do have hidden emotional practices, other practices have more of a sense of trickery such as deception and fake news.

Deception

When attending a magic show people expect to be tricked, but possibly not in an online seminar. With magic it is clear that deception occurs through distraction and changing perception of what is occurring. To some extent this is also the case when being deceived in higher education. Few people anticipate deception in a learning environment and therefore when they are tricked this can result in anger and frustration. Emotional and cognitive disjunction of the deception undertaken by Taras and Steel demonstrates this (Taras & Steel, 2007). The students were told by Taras that their usual lecturer was suspended in a sympathetic way and explained to the students there would be some changes in the assessment. The students complained, so Taras provided a signup sheet for them to join a union and take their complaints further; then watched as the students came together as a group to take action. The students were later debriefed about the deception with lectures illustrating to them how easy it was to violate trust and psychological contracts. A further example of this was a study that included the use of pedagogical agents within an online problem-based learning (PBL) seminar series (Savin-Baden et al., 2016). A pedagogical agent (or chatbot) is a software application that can provide a human-like interaction using a natural language interface. Examples of these are Siri, Cortana, Alexa or the virtual online assistants found on some websites, such as Anna on the Ikea website. The passive detection test is where participants are not primed to the potential presence of a pedagogical agent within online PBL. The active detection test is where participants are primed to the potential presence of a pedagogical agent. The study used PBL online, so as to give a focus for discussions and participation, without creating too much artificiality. Students, in the main, did not detect the agent, and the ways in which students positioned the agent tended to influence the interaction between them. Thus, those who assumed the agent was an incompetent student ignored him and those who believed he had language difficulties felt sorry for him. Students' positioning of the agent – as shy, arrogant and confused was largely a mechanism used for rationalising their feelings that something was awry or uncanny.

Fake News and Fake Representation

Fake news was a term that was popularised during the 2016 US elections in order to describe both inaccurate news and staged news shows. It is an important concern for students to be aware of when learning in higher education. Kathrin Otrel-Cass and Fasching (2021) explored young people's encounters with fake news and found that in order to enable them to understand the potential instances of dupery, teaching in this area needed to be personalised to reflect students' experiences of online and fake news. Özdan (2021) explored whether legal remedies against the circulation and publication of fake news were in fact compatible with international human rights law. His findings indicated that when dealing with fake news, policy makers should adopt reason and should expect conformity that upholds with principles of international human rights law. Further he suggests that the policy of censorship is not the solution, but instead media literacy programmes and transparency policies need to be adopted (p. 93).

In the 2020s the growth of large language models and the use of artificial intelligence (AI) to create and change images is a further concern. The stealing and reuse of data and images is invariably something few people consider in terms of the impact on artists' revenues and the scraping of data from people's Facebook and Instagram accounts. Thus we all need to understand how to deal with identity issues online and be encouraged to manage and control the information contained in our online networks.

Algorithmic Imaginaries

Bucher defines the algorithmic imaginary as the 'way of thinking about what algorithms are, what they should be, how they function and what these imaginations in turn make possible' (Bucher, 2018, p. 40). Algorithms are created by humans and the reproduction of world views and stereotypes are, as it were, 'designed in' by humans. A further concern is assumptions that are made by humans about the impact and control algorithms may have on our lives. An example of this assumed influence is provided by Singler.

Singler explored tweets that mention the phrase 'blessed by the algorithm' in order to examine popular concepts of AI as divinity (Singler, 2020). The phrase is used by people to suggest that they have been fortunate in receiving content fed to them on social media platforms, whether in terms of affirmation or jobs offered or suggested. Singler found seven types of tweets about being blessed by the algorithm, these included:

1. User hope of being blessed by the algorithm
2. Response to recommendation for that day such as music and shopping

3. Being blessed by finding work through gig economy job – the term 'gig economy' refers to small tasks or jobs (the 'gigs') that individuals are contracted to carry out. These jobs are allocated digitally, invariably through algorithmic management methods (Tassinari & Maccarone, 2020)
4. Just saying or feeling blessed by the algorithm in a vague unconnected way
5. Using religious language by non-religion people to argue for being blessed
6. Negative responses such as being cynical about the current state of affairs or people's successes
7. References to science fiction characters, concepts and plotlines.

What is particularly interesting about both the idea of being blessed by the algorithm and the way in which tweets are used is that there is an assumption of blessing, beginning with an assumption that blessing through AI technology is not only a possibility but a reality. As MacKenzie and Bhatt (2020, p. 9) argue:

> The digital is now 'integrated and imbricated with our everyday actions and interactions' (Feenberg, 2019, p. 8). Its structures and divisions, mediated by human behaviour but exacerbated by … algorithms, are the very drivers which shape the conditions of knowledge production, circulation, and consumption … the documentary-drama, The Social Dilemma (Orlowski, 2020), offers a powerful explanation of how these systems operate to manipulate our beliefs and behaviours.

What is also of ethical concern is the impact of algorithms and the use of large language models on the environment.

ENVIRONMENTAL ETHICS

There are a range of views about what should be done about caring for the environment, with some people arguing change must happen but that it is too expensive, whilst others suggest that adaptation rather than mitigation is the only realistic way forward. Mann has argued that we are facing a new climate war because of the number of sceptical stances, he explains:

> The most hard-core contingent - the deniers - are, as we have seen, in the process of going extinct (though there is still a remnant population of them). They are being replaced by other breeds of deceivers and dissemblers, namely, downplayers, deflectors, dividers, delayers, and doomers-willing participants in a multipronged strategy seeking to deflect blame, divide the public, delay action by promoting "alternative" solutions that don't actually solve the problem, or insist we simply accept our fate-it's too late to do anything about it anyway, so we might as well keep the oil flowing. The climate wars have thus not ended. They have simply evolved into a new climate war.
>
> *(Mann, 2021, p. 45)*

An example of this can be seen in The Global Warming Policy Foundation in the UK, founded by former Conservative Chancellor Nigel Lawson. The group promotes a sceptical stance towards climate change, and this is fostered through a strong group within the Conservative Party in the UK. Some of the questions that need to be considered are not just how green businesses, universities, colleges and churches are, but how ethical their practices are, even those that may be hidden such as the source of goods and hardware. For example, there is little exploration of the ethics of computer hardware manufacture and much of the hardware is bought because it is cheap rather than ethically sourced. The materials used for buildings in terms of the extent to which they are locally sourced and environmentally friendly need to be considered, as does the heating used within buildings and generally the extent of our use of renewable energy. To date relatively few institutions, businesses and churches use solar power, ground source heat pumps or wind power. Other areas that need to be addressed include purchasing fair-trade food, sustainable fish and locally sourced food and increasing our use of fair-trade technology.

POSTDIGITAL ETHICS AND THEOLOGY: DEFRACTURING AND RECONNECTING

John and I (Savin-Baden & Reader, 2022) explored the location of God within a postdigital cosmos, specifically how our postdigital condition might affect our views of theistic belief, spirituality and transcendence. We argued that theology must develop in the light of the challenges and yet at the same time we must guard against the notion that technology is simply something we use or deploy in an instrumental fashion. This section builds on this discussion, suggesting the need for refracturing and reconnecting.

One of the somewhat understated or ignored difficulties with digitalisation is that it tends to divide knowledge, concepts and ideas. Digitisation is defined here as a division of knowledge into two discrete units which are valued more than models of knowledge which connect human experience (following Trozzo, 2022). The creation of such silos results in covert surveillance and fake news. Divisions and silos therefore result in the ethical conundrums about how ethical decisions can be made that locate and situate human experience in context. Trozzo suggests

> … theology is a work of defracturing or reconnecting forms of human knowledge in weaving together a coherent narrative of human experience that provides hope for relationality in the midst of the destructive tendencies at play in the world.
>
> *(p. 91)*

When discussing ethics and as a result of these divisions and silos, the structures that support them are often forgotten. Furthermore, the impact of digitisation on labour in manufacturing, the environment, energy production, production of materials and human well-being are often omitted in discussions about postdigital ethics. The risk, as Trozzo suggests, the need to defracture and reconnect so that postdigital ethics can be used to highlight the siloed space is created through digitisation. The way forward is, as Trozzo suggests, to embrace digital theology which is 'not about online content but rather planetary interconnections' (p. 97). Based on the work of Trozzo, Table 1.2 provides ways in which postdigital theologies can inform new ways of considering postdigital ethics.

TABLE 1.2
Postdigital theologies and postdigital ethics

Element	Definition	Application to postdigital ethics
Mythos thinking	Thinking which connects knowledge and acknowledges planetary connections	The sense of the need to be more imaginative in terms of relating to one another and caring for the needs of the planet
Materialism	This considers the nexus of the digital with the social effects of capitalism and climate change	A recognition of the need to engage in debates about the socio-political impact of the postdigital
Multiplicities	There is acknowledgement of multiple stances, subjects and views in postdigital theologies and ethics	The recognitions of the merging of the digital into and across complex spaces that interrupt traditional ethical stances
Transcendence	The seeking of encounter with the divine through new forms of knowledge in the postdigital world	A realisation of the importance of the interconnection of relationships and co-becoming that affects a person's engagement with the digital

However, what is important is the consideration of what might be done in terms of practical responses to ethical concerns and ways of dealing with possible (un)ethical technologies.

PRACTICAL ETHICAL CONCERNS

Postdigital ethics also introduces questions about human labour and the questionable manufacturing conditions in China (Qiu, 2016), Kenya (Lee, 2018) and elsewhere. The hours are long, the activities repetitive and routine and the wages are low. Qiu (2016) compares the 17th-century transatlantic slave trade with the iSlaves of the 21st century. The iSlaves, Qiu uses as an example, are the Chinese workers at Foxconn, an electronics company whose largest buyer is Apple. Qiu notes that student interns are paid below the minimum wage, legally supported by the Chinese Government. The challenge from Qiu is that there is a need to rethink our relationship with digital technologies. Further, as Lee (2018) points out, 'the information prepared here forms a crucial part of some of Silicon Valley's biggest and most famous efforts in AI'. Unseen labour also involves working with data, as Andrejevic et al. note:

> If one of the casualties of a fascination with the 'virtual' character of software, applications, code, and data has been a shift away from political-economic approaches to the media, the reliance of data mining on capital-intensive infrastructure reminds us of the ongoing salience of political-economic concerns.
>
> *(Andrejevic et al., 2015, p. 385)*

Our sites of production may not be ethical, but as Jandrić (2019) points out, biases are not carried through cultures and people creating technology, biases are built into technology in ways that are unpredictable. This in turn raises further questions about the use of machine learning which is essentially designed to enable computers to act without being programmed.

Ethical concerns in the field of machine learning can be considered in relation to robotics ethics, machine morality and intimacy ethics. For example:

- Robot ethics needs to examine ethical questions about how humans should design, deploy and treat robots.
- Machine morality introduces questions about the moral capacities a robot or virtual human should have and how these might be implemented.
- Intimacy ethics explores how engaging with virtual humans can offer people opportunities to connect with something emotionally and feel supported, even loved, without the need to reciprocate.

Thus some of the ethical issues are that whilst ethical behaviour needs to be 'designed-in' to virtual humans, however, designing appropriate and effective ethics standards are complex and far reaching. For example, if autonomous combat robots or AIs are deployed by the military whose fault is it if they mistakenly attack or fail to distinguish correct targets? What is most important here is that the legal context is ever-changing, and thus research for a digital age, in some respects, requires researchers to be aware of current debates and so plan research projects and data management accordingly, as well as being aware of issues of surveillance.

LOCATING POSTDIGITAL ETHICAL FUTURES

This section considers a few of the possibilities for resistance to the rapidly moving changes that are affecting our world, suggesting ways in which it might be possible to take a stance towards some of the difficulties we face.

Opportunities for Resistance

As is mentioned in Chapter 2, Coeckelbergh and Reader argue that AI also presents opportunities for resistance:

> We can resist, and we can "hack" the technology. Not all of us have a technical background, but we can use the technology in a different way than it's meant, if that helps us to live more meaningful lives.
>
> *(Coeckelbergh & Reader, 2025, page number will be needed)*

John Reader and I talked often about how technology affected us, his argument was always that it was something that managed and manoeuvred us, invariably without us knowing. My argument was that we always had a choice. I believe we still do. Resistance does not mean closing down everything digital, turning off the machines forever, but instead realising and recognising how we can manage it, rather than it managing us.

Questioning the Use of Large Language Models

The growth in the use of Large Language models (LLMs) in higher education is currently assumed to be detrimental to student learning and academic integrity. LLMs are also perceived to be affecting societal values about the nature of learning and education. The current assumption about the use of LLMs is that they compromise learning and academic integrity (Weissman, 2023). However, to date, there is little research that indicates whether LLMs actually help or hinder learning and academic integrity (Rudolph et al., 2023). Further, evidence suggests that up to one-fifth of students worldwide are using AI in assessments (Cassidy, 2023), yet as Sullivan et al. (2023) note, academics do not as yet see LLMs as a significant threat to higher education. In terms of theology, Dimara et al. (2024) suggest that theological doctrines shape perspectives on AI, but today there is little if any research on the impact of AI in theological education. Authors such as Graves (2023) suggest LLMs such as ChatGPT can be trained to support theological research and the development of sermons. However, such suggestions introduce questions about academic and theological integrity and the nature of theological authority. As Schwarting (2023) argues 'LLMs do not carry the attribution associated with authorship, or the agency associated with personhood'. There are also concerns about using ChatGPT since its data set has been created through scraping material from many sites, largely illegally.

Shifting Ethical Stances

The engagement of society in virtue and modest ethics is a colossal undertaking which will require seismic shifts. Suggestions here are elementary but the wider discussion in this volume might be the beginnings of a new ethics manifesto for the future, as Brown argues

> … that a recovery of the language of virtue, community, tradition, character, and so on, as counterweights to the dominant narrative of individualism and markets, might help us to articulate aspects of what is essentially human, and thus inform technological developments in which the human and the technology are less and less distinguishable
>
> *(Brown, 2021, pp. 133–134)*

In practice this means living a life of constantly questioning our practices – the ways time is spent, what is bought, what is shared and the ways in which we can stand against capitalism and the management of ourselves by unseen entities.

CONCLUSION

This chapter has begun the work of mapping the landscape of postdigital ethics by suggesting that postdigital ethics then brings together traditional ethical theories, but also introduces newer stances towards ethics such as modest ethics. It has offered a broad overview of some of the concerns related to postdigital ethics, designed as it were to be a jumping-off point for the rest of the text.

REFERENCES

Andrejevic, M., Hearn, A., & Kennedy, H. (2015). Cultural studies of data mining: introduction. *European Journal of Cultural Studies*, *18*(4–5), 379–394. https://doi.org/10.1177/1367549415577395.

Brown, M. (2021). Ethics, character, and community: Moral formation and modelling the human. In M. Savin-Baden (Ed.), *Postdigital Humans: Transitions, transformations and transcendence* (pp. 125–140). Cham Switzerland: Springer International Publishing. https://doi.org/10.1007/978-3-030-65592-1_8

Bucher, T. (2018). *If… then: Algorithmic power and politics*. New York: Oxford University Press.

Calhoun, A. W., Pian-Smith, M. C. M., Truog, R. D., Gaba, D. M., & Meyer, E. C. (2015). Deception and simulation education: Issues, concepts, and commentary. *Simulation in Healthcare*, 10(3), 163–169.

Cassidy, C. (2023, January 17). Lecturer detects bot-use in one fifth of assessments as concerns mount over AI in exams. *The Guardian*. https://www.theguardian.com/australia-news/2023/jan/17/lecturer-detects-bot-use-in-one-fifth-of-assessments-as-concerns-mount-over-ai-in-exams

Coeckelbergh, M., & Reader, J. (2025). Searching for the good life: Boundary crossing, co-existence, and conviviality. In M. Savin-Baden, M. Power, & J. Reader (Eds.), *Postdigital ethical futures: Essays in honour of John Reader*. Routledge.

Dimara, V., Chatzivasileiou, D., Psomiadi, A., Efthymiou-Egleton, T. W., Kassar, L., & Gancas, H. (2024). Artificial intelligence and theology: Can different doctrines have different outcomes? *Journal of Politics and Ethics in New Technologies and AI*, 3(1), e37714–e37714. https://ejournals.epublishing.ekt.gr/index.php/jpentai/article/view/37714

Evans, A. (2025). Modest ethics. In M. Savin-Baden, M. Power, & J. Reader (Eds.), *Postdigital ethical futures: Essays in honour of John Reader*. pp. 16–27. Abingdon, Oxon CRC Press: Routledge.

Feenberg, A. (2019). Postdigital or predigital? *Postdigital Science and Education*, 1(1), 8–9. https://link.springer.com/content/pdf/10.1007/s42438-018-0027-2.pdf

Graves, M. (2023). ChatGPT's significance for theology. *Theology and Science*, 21(2), 201–204. https://doi.org/10.1080/14746700.2023.2186345

Jandrić, P. (2019). The postdigital challenge of critical media literacy. *The International Journal of Critical Media Literacy*, 1(1), 26–37.

Jandrić, P., Knox, J., Besley, T., Ryberg, T., Suoranta, J., & Hayes, S. (2018). Postdigital science and education. *Educational Philosophy and Theory*, 50(10)893–899.

Latour, B. (1987). *Science in action: How to follow scientists and engineers through society*. Cambridge, MA: Harvard University Press.

Lee, D. (2018, November 3). Why big tech pays poor Kenyans to teach self-driving cars. *BBC Technology*. https://www.bbc.com/news/technology-46055595. Accessed 15 October 2024.

MacKenzie, A., & Bhatt, I. (2020). Lies, bullshit and fake news: Some epistemological concerns. In *Postdigital science and education* (Vol. 2, Issue 1, pp. 9–13). Cham: Springer International Publishing. https://doi.org/10.1007/s42438-018-0025-4

Mann, M. E. (2021). *The new climate war: The fight to take back our planet*. PublicAffairs.

Orlowski, J. (2020). *The social dilemma* [Documentary Film]. Los Gatos, CA: Netfix.

Otrel-Cass, K., & Fasching, M. (2021). Postdigital truths: Educational reflections on fake news and digital identities. In M. Savin-Baden (Ed.), *Postdigital humans: Transitions, transformations and transcendence* (pp. 89–108). Cham: Springer International Publishing. https://doi.org/10.1007/978-3-030-65592-1_6

Özdan, S. (2021). The right to freedom of expression versus legal actions against fake news: A case study of Singapore. In A. MacKenzie, J. Rose, & I. Bhatt (Eds.), *The epistemology of deceit in a postdigital era: Dupery by design* (pp. 77–94). Cham: Springer International Publishing. https://doi.org/10.1007/978-3-030-72154-1_5

Popper, K. (1959). *The logic of scientific discovery.* London: Hutchinson.

Qiu, J. L. (2016). *Goodbye iSlave: A digital manifesto.* Urbana, IL: University of Illinois Press.

Reader, J., & Evans, A. (2019). *Ethics after new materialism: A modest undertaking.* Rochdale, UK: William Temple Foundation.

Reader, J., & Savin-Baden, M. (2020). Ethical conundrums and virtual humans. *Postdigital Science and Education*, 2(2), 289–301. https://doi.org/10.1007/s42438-019-00095-2

Rudolph, J., Tan, S., & Tan, S. (2023). ChatGPT: Bullshit spewer or the end of traditional assessments in higher education? *Journal of Applied Learning and Teaching*, 6(1), 1–22. https://doi.org/10.37074/jalt.2023.6.1.9

Savin-Baden, M., Bhakta, R., & Burden, D. (2016). Cyber enigmas? Passive detection and Pedagogical agents: Can students spot the fake? *Proceedings of the 10th International Conference on Networked Learning 2016*, Edinburgh, pp. 456–463.

Savin-Baden, M., & Reader, J. (Eds.). (2022). *Postdigital theologies: Technology, belief, and practice.* Cham: Springer Nature.

Schwarting, M. (2023, June 10). To Christians developing LLM applications: A warning, and some suggestions. *AI & Faith.* https://aiandfaith.org/to-christians-developing-llm-applications-a-warning-and-some-suggestions/

Shakespeare, W. (1594). *The comedy of errors.* Oxford: Oxford University Press.

Shakespeare, W. (1605). *A midsummer night's dream.* Oxford: Oxford University Press.

Sinclair, C. (2021). Learning from the Dupers: Showing the workings. In A. MacKenzie, J. Alison, & I. Rose (Eds.), *The epistemology of deceit in a postdigital era: Dupery by design* (pp. 233–249). Cham: Springer International Publishing. https://doi.org/10.1007/978-3-030-72154-1_13

Singler, B. (2020). "Blessed by the algorithm": Theistic conceptions of artificial intelligence in online discourse. *AI & Society*, 35(4), 945–955.

Sullivan, M., Kelly, A., & McLaughlan, P. (2023). ChatGPT in higher education: Considerations for academic integrity and student learning. *Journal of Applied Learning & Teaching*, 6(1), 1–10. https://doi.org/10.37074/jalt.2023.6.1.17

Tassinari, A., & Maccarone, V. (2020). "Riders on the Storm: Workplace oslidarity among Gig economy couriers in Italy and the UK. *Journal Work Employment and Society*, *34*(1), 35–54.

Taras, D., & Steel, P. (2007). We provoked business students to unionize: Using deception to prove an IR point. *British Journal of Industrial Relations*, 45(1), 179–198.

Trozzo, E. (2022). Mythos and postdigital theology: Beyond the limits of digitalization. *Khazanah Theologia*, 4(2), 91–102. https://doi.org/10.15575/kt.v4i2.19591

Weissman, J. (2023, February 9). ChatGPT is a plague upon education. *Inside Higher Ed.* https://www.insidehighered.com/views/2023/02/09/chatgpt-plague-upon-education-opinion

2 A New Materialist Approach to Postdigital Ethics

Adrian Evans and John Reader

INTRODUCTION

In this chapter we argue that a new type of ethics is needed to deal with the complexities of our postdigital lives. To set the context, we begin with two short stories to illustrate the ways in which digital technologies are fundamentally altering our everyday realities. We then offer different definitions of the digital and postdigital, and we contend that certain, particularly compelling, definitions of the latter point to a need for renewed ethical attention and conceptual innovation. Next, we outline our understanding of New Materialism and the types of 'modest' and more-than-human ethics that derive from New Materialist approaches. Finally, we identify three key lines of enquiry that we believe a New Materialist inspired ethics might open-up in relation to helping us deal with the ethical complexities and novelties of our postdigital lives. These include a focus on 'techno-ethics' and the ways in which values and power relations become embedded in technologies; a focus on the ethics of interfaces rather than the ethics of subjects and objects and a focus on the performativity (or world making capacity) of digital technologies and digital modes of representation. The ideas that inform this chapter have developed from many conversations between John Reader and me. John pioneered the use of New Materialist ideas within theological and ethical contexts, and his contributions to this field will be profoundly missed. In writing this chapter I have endeavoured to stay true to the spirit of John's approach both to ethics and to the postdigital but I cannot hope to recreate this chapter as it would have been with John's continuing input and it is far less rich as a result. Nevertheless, I hope that the ideas stay true to John's vision and to his desire for intellectual experimentation.

CONTEXT

We would like to begin with two short stories, or perhaps one might even call them parables, that serve to illustrate both the ubiquitous presence of digital technologies in our everyday lives and the types of moral and ethical upheavals that these technologies are engendering.

 DOI: 10.1201/9781003497950-3

Our first story begins on the morning of 1 September 1859 on the outskirts of London when the amateur astronomer Richard Carrington observed two patches of bright white light erupting from dark spots on the surface of the sun (Clark, 2007). Later that day the full effects of this geomagnetic storm were realised as telegraph systems failed throughout the world, in some cases giving operators electric shocks and causing fires in telegraph stations. This geomagnetic storm was subsequently dubbed the 'Carrington Event' and it has become an important benchmark for assessing the likely impacts of space weather. If a similar event occurred today, in our electrified, digitised and computerised world the results could be disastrous, severely impacting satellites, GPS, power grids and the Internet. Indeed, a workshop report by the US National Academies of Sciences, Engineering and Medicine predicted that such an event could cause between 1 and 2 trillion dollars' worth of damage (National Research Council, 2008).

Our second story concerns a murder that took place in Southern Japan in 2008, when a middle-aged piano teacher snapped and killed her husband following the souring of their relationship (see McNeill, 2008). A tragic but relatively unremarkable story, except that in this case the 'murder' did not involve the killing of a flesh and blood human but rather the deletion of a virtual character. In fact, the couple was only 'married' within the virtual world of 'MapleStory', an online environment in which users are encouraged to travel around alternative worlds and engage in virtual relationships. After a falling out, the piano teacher hacked into her virtual husband's online account and deleted his 'Maple Story' persona. The woman was arrested, not for digital murder, but for illegally using her husband's ID to access his computer, however the story sparked a broader debate amongst online communities about the legal status of digital assets and whether virtual crimes should face real-world punishments (Rumbles, 2011).

These stories serve to illustrate two important points. First, they show the extent to which digital technologies saturate our lives. We see this in relation to the Carrington event and in the disruptive potential of future space weather to wreak economic, social and environmental havoc upon a world that has become dependent on digital technologies as a ubiquitous background to our lives, practices and competencies. Second, they demonstrate the extent to which our current legal and ethical frameworks are ill-equipped to deal with the intertwining of our digital and everyday lives. The transformative impact of the adoption of a range of digital technologies forces us to rethink even our most basic legal notions of agency, property and personhood.

The vast majority of our ethical and moral frameworks, be they deontological, utilitarian or virtue based, place the human at the centre of their concerns. Deontological frameworks tell humans what they should and should not do, utilitarian frameworks weigh up the outcomes of actions in terms of their impacts on humans (or on other entities valued by and often valuable for humans) and virtue ethics concerns itself with sculpting improved human characters. Yet, we live in a world in which humans, or at least humans acting alone, are no longer central to decision-making. Humans act alongside, are guided by, are enabled and disabled by technologies, especially digital technologies. We live in a more-than-human world in which the agency of non-human actors continues to increase. One possible way forward to adequately address these fundamental changes is to explore new theoretical resources that are more suited to dealing with the complexities of our digital and postdigital lives. We argue that one such theoretical resource can be found in New Materialism and the types of modest ethics that we believe emerge from New Materialist approaches (Reader, 2017; Reader & Evans, 2019).

DEFINING THE DIGITAL AND POSTDIGITAL

There are several different definitions of the digital, indeed the *Oxford English Dictionary* lists 19 different meanings of the word and even recognises the phrase 'born-digital' for content that has never existed in an analogue format (Oxford English Dictionary, 1989). It is worth briefly highlighting three of these definitions, as they bring out important and contrasting dimensions of this term and foreshadow some of our conceptual arguments later in the chapter. First, the digital can refer in a broad sense to the use of electronic technology and especially the use of computers. Second, the digital can refer to the use of either/or, zero/one signals in contrast to the continuous waves of analogue transmissions. This is an interesting dimension of the digital as it alludes to not only the purity and relative incorruptibility of digital transmissions, but also to the precise and unyielding nature of digital representation and information processing. Third, the digital can refer to fingers or toes (from the original Latin 'digitus'). As we shall see, this particular meaning, which grounds the digital in embodied experience, is of particular, albeit tangential, relevance to our modest ethics approach, which also highlights the importance of understanding our embodied interactions with digital technologies.

There has been a vast amount of academic research and broader commentary on the nature of the digital and the types of social, cultural and economic transformations that digital technologies have engendered. This ranges from the business-focused analysis of how best to leverage digital technologies for commercial success, by, for example, using the Internet of Things to improve supply chain efficiency and transparency (see Dörner & Edelman, 2015) to the more socio-cultural-focused analysis of authors such as Felix Stadler, who has contrasted our current 'digital condition' to McLuhan's 'Guttenberg Galaxy' and focused attention on the impact of digital technologies on democracy and technological sovereignty (Stalder, 2018).

More recently, authors have also begun to use the term 'postdigital' as a novel analytical concept for interrogating our relationship with digital technologies and our embeddedness in digital cultures (Cramer, 2015; Savin-Baden & Reader, 2022). There are two major strands of thought within the 'postdigital', in the first the postdigital is defined as a rejection of modern technologies and a return to older pre-technological ways of living. This has been brought about by the failures of the initial utopian visions of freedom and openness that digital technologies seemed to offer and the increasing use of digital technologies for surveillance, control and marketing. Seen in this light the postdigital also involves adopting a more humanistic approach to solving problems with a reduced focus on numerical analysis and computerised solutions. As Cramer (2015, p. 12) states: 'Typewriters are not the only medium which has recently been resurrected as literally a post-digital device: other examples include vinyl records, and more recently also audio cassettes, as well as analogue photography and artists' printmaking'.

In the second strand of thought the concept of the postdigital implies an acceptance of the fact that the digital has become so interconnected with contemporary life that it no longer makes sense to separate the digital from the non-digital. As Jandrić et al. (2018, p. 893) state: 'We are increasingly no longer in a world where digital technology and media is separate, virtual, "other" to a "natural" human and social life'. Furthermore, as Negroponte (1998) states: 'Like air and drinking water, being digital will be noticed only by its absence, not its presence'.

In this version of the postdigital the 'post' symbolises the transcendence of previous digital versus non-digital dualisms rather than a simple rejection of the digital. It is this version that most resonates with our understandings of the status of the digital in contemporary culture, and it is this version that we believe is best suited to depict the modern realities of our complex and materially, technologically and digitally entangled lives. However, it is also this interpretation of the postdigital that presents the greatest challenges to our traditional ethical, moral and legal frameworks; primarily because it decentres the human as the principal locus of ethical agency. How, for example, can we apportion blame and attribute responsibility in a postdigital world when an autonomous vehicle crashes? How can we deal with future postdigital murders when the victims are not just online personas but digital twins who co-evolved with their fleshy siblings from birth? How can we continue to promote democracy in the context of weaponised social media? How can we cling to concepts of human agency and autonomy when our lives have become so intensely monitored, measured, scripted and nudged by digital technologies? In short, how can we still hope to use ethical frameworks developed in the pre-digital era to adequately address the novel ethical issues arising in a postdigital world?

One potential solution to these problems is to adapt and reformulate the same ethical frameworks that have served us so well for decades, centuries and millennia. We can extend deontological rules to recognise and incorporate new digital crimes and misdemeanours and we can adjust the locus of utilitarian evaluations to incorporate informational and digital assets (see, e.g., Floridi, 1999). These are valid approaches that yield interesting insights; however, they do not exhaust the field of ethical enquiry and we believe that they can be complemented by alternative ethical approaches that appear well-suited to confront the challenges that we have discussed. We believe that one such alternative ethical approach can be derived from New Materialism (Reader, 2017). In the next sections, we continue to develop this argument by outlining our understanding of New Materialism and by considering how the modest ethical ideas derived from this approach could provoke new questions and open up new lines of enquiry into the ethics of the digital.

THE MODEST ETHICS OF NEW MATERIALISM

In this section we provide a brief summary of some of the key ideas of a range of scholars who have contributed to a comprehensive rethinking of the role of materiality in our social, cultural and economic lives (for a more detailed analysis, see Reader, 2017). This rethinking has been partly prompted by intellectual reasons, such as a desire to move beyond traditional Cartesian and representationalist forms of understanding, and partly prompted by a desire to adequately conceptualise the fundamental changes that have occurred in our social and cultural lives, brought about at least in part by technological and digital innovations. Our aim is not to provide a comprehensive account of New Materialist ideas, or to strictly define or limit what might count as a New Materialist approach, instead we adopt a pragmatic approach to creatively connect the ideas of certain key authors, all of whom have changed the ways in which we think about materialities and some of whom would be more content with the 'New Materialist' label than others.

New Materialist authors form a diverse collective, including posthumanists, such as Donna Haraway (2013), speculative realists, such as Quentin Meillassoux (2010), Anthropologists, such as Tim Ingold (2021), vitalists, such as Deleuze (2004) and Philosophers of Science, such as Isabelle Stengers (2018), nevertheless they share some core beliefs (Coole & Frost, 2010). First, they adopt a posthumanist conception of matter as lively or exhibiting agency (see, e.g., Bennett, 2020). They also view matter as active, productive and resilient. As Reader (2017, p. 3) states: 'So rather than matter being seen as inert or passive 'stuff' that requires an external form in order to exist in a concrete way, matter is reinterpreted as self-organising and matter-energy'. Second, they seek to move beyond the cultural turn, which placed an emphasis on language, discourse and values, to re-engage with the material realities of everyday life. Third, they show a desire to (critically but open-mindedly) engage with recent developments in the natural sciences and their impact on society. For example, many New Materialist authors have discussed the implications of post-classical physics, which views matter in terms of elusive quanta and fields rather than fixed point particles. Furthermore, New Materialists have sought to address the types of complex bio-political and bio-ethical issues that have arisen from technological developments in the biological and medical sciences, including the genetic modification/editing of crops and animals, stem cell research and synthetic biology.

In the remainder of this section, we would like to illustrate some of the distinctive characteristics of New Materialist thought by drawing on the writings of two key authors, namely Gilles Deleuze and Bruno Latour. Whilst Deleuze might be best characterised as a vitalist philosopher, it is clear that his writings have had a profound impact on New Materialism and in particular on the works of prominent New Materialist authors, such as Braidotti (2013), Delanda (2013), Bennett (2020) and Bryant (2011). Deleuze's thought is complex and multifaceted and he has introduced the world to a rich variety of new concepts, including the body without organs, deterritorialisation, multiplicity and difference. He has also offered innovative and alternative conceptualisations of materiality and ethics. For example, his concept of 'order words', developed in his book 'The Logic of Sense', outlines how materiality and meaning are inextricably linked together, as he contends that enunciative assemblages are always linked to material assemblages of bodies, passions and actions (Deleuze, 2004). Language and sign systems in Deleuze's view do not primarily function to provide information or aid communication, but rather to issue imperatives or commands that order the material world. Seen in this fashion Deleuze moves away from Cartesian dualisms of mind and body and places materialities and meanings together on a flatter ontological plane, which in turn has ramifications for human agency and the material dependence of human thought and action. Similarly, Deleuze and Guattari's concept of 'becoming' and their privileging of relationality over discrete and separated subjects and objects have opened up new avenues of enquiry (Deleuze & Guattari, 1987). In particular, the concept highlights the interconnectivity of materials and life forms as they co-evolve in assemblages. For example, it makes little sense to consider the evolution of wasps and orchids as separate biological identities, as they are 'locked in a block of becoming' from which they cannot easily escape.

Finally, and perhaps most importantly in relation to ethical considerations, Deleuze contends that ethics are bound up with the movement of events (Deleuze, 2004). Drawing on influences from Spinoza and from the Stoic's concept of destiny, Deleuze contends that ethics is not so much about living a 'good life', as one cannot know that until it has been lived anyway, but about making oneself worthy of the event. This provides a stark contrast to mainstream ethical frameworks that place human beings and human agency at the centre of ethical concerns and as the key locus of ethical responsibility. Within Deleuzian ethics, humans cannot control events, but rather they can only seek to affirm, enhance or intensify those events.

The second author we would like to discuss is Bruno Latour. Similar to Deleuze, Latour provides us with a range of conceptual resources for rethinking materialities and their relationships to ethical issues (Latour, 2007). Latour contended that material objects are shot through with human and societal values and that there is a circular relationship between technology and society. This is because technological artefacts are never purely technical but emerge from a specific social context and embody/materialise social values. Furthermore, technological objects do not have neutral social outcomes rather they configure their users in certain ways.

Latour also contended that in the West there has been an artificially imposed division between nature on the one hand and culture on the other (Latour, 2004). Nature is seen as the realm of inert objects responding to casual laws and processes, and culture is seen as the domain of human subjects, values and morality. This is problematic because it means that democracy can only be applied to one side of the divide. There can be no debate, argument, discussion or negotiation in the face of scientifically proven 'matters of fact'. However, it is precisely these 'matters of fact' that Latour takes issue with. He believes that a lot of debate, discussion, disagreement and the reconciling of alternative models and perspectives does indeed occur within scientific communities. However, these uncertainties are too frequently covered over and hidden from broader democratic and deliberative processes, as scientists only enter the broader public debate to produce facts and close down arguments rather than to embrace uncertainties and to make them public and open to broader scrutiny. In contrast to this division between nature and culture; between science and politics and between objects and humans, Latour wants to replace it with a single community or collective of humans and non-humans. This in turn has significant implications both for our understanding of materialities and for our understanding of the scope and subject matter of what can count as ethics. Indeed, seen in this way, ethics do not just reside in human thought and reflection but rather are carried in and emergent from complex assemblages of humans and non-humans, signs and materialities.

Thus, one can see that scholars such as Latour and Deleuze provide us with a radically new conceptualisation of the material and the role of materialities in our social, cultural and economic lives. Moreover, they point the way to an alternative version of ethics that is more suited to cope with both our new scientific and academic understandings of materiality and the new types of material, technological and digital artefacts that surround us in the 21st century. In a previous publication (Reader & Evans, 2019) we coined the term 'modest ethics' to describe some of the ethical insights emerging from New Materialism. We believe that New Materialist ethics are modest as they focus on the worldly, material and embodied dimensions of events and occurrences, furthermore they decentre the importance of human agency as the sole driver and arbiter of ethical actions. In the next section we discuss how these 'modest ethics' might be applied to the postdigital.

TOWARDS A MODEST ETHICS OF THE POSTDIGITAL

Throughout this chapter we have argued that our postdigital culture generates many new ethical considerations that cannot be easily addressed by traditional deontological, utilitarian or virtue-based approaches to ethics. Furthermore, we have suggested that one potentially productive way forward would be to draw on the resources of New Materialist thinkers to help us navigate the complexities and novelties of our postdigital world. Unlike traditional ethical approaches, we would contend that New Materialism offers a modest approach to ethics that is rooted in everyday life and in our day-to-day, specific and situated encounters with technologies, objects, environments and other humans. Furthermore, a New Materialist approach would conceptualise ethics as emerging from and bounded by these situated encounters rather than something that necessarily has broader transcendental relevance across different contexts. In this section we would like to propose three key lines of enquiry that we believe a New Materialist-inspired 'modest ethics' would open-up; these include a focus on *techno-ethics*, a focus on *ethical interfaces* and a focus on *digital performativity*.

Techno-ethics

We use the term 'techno-ethics' to describe the ways in which ethical values and power relations become embedded in technologies. Technologies, and perhaps especially digital technologies, are never value-free but rather are embedded in the social and ethical milieu from which they arise. In designing a technology, digital or otherwise, designers are responding to a perceived social demand and a perceived economic market. They also make a set of assumptions about how the new technology will be used and the types of individuals who will be using it. Furthermore, new technologies do not emerge in a vacuum and they are often intended to replace past practices and past technologies; automobiles replace horse-driven carriages, word processors replace typewriters and tractors replace oxen. As a result, seemingly novel designs often continue to bear the marks of past designs and past practical, social and ethical considerations.

Whilst the intertwining of technology and ethics has a long history (Stiegler, 1998), it is clear that digital technologies offer new ways to materialise values and assumptions about social life. For example, assumptions about the types and heights of users are incorporated into the programming of automatic sliding doors; algorithms are often coded by men along with tacit expectations that men will be the main end-users and PowerPoint slides are designed based on sets of assumptions about what makes a good presentation. Of course, some would argue that these are human values that are designed into technologies by humans and, as such, we can use traditional ethical approaches to evaluate them. Whilst this is to some extent true, it is also clear that materials and technologies cannot act as transparent mediums for the extension of human will. In other words, the act of materialising and objectifying values creates new and emergent issues of an ethical-material-social nature.

As well as materialising ethical values, digital technologies can also script, configure and 'nudge' their end-users in potentially problematic ways. Video game designers invest a lot of time and effort in making their games as visually and emotionally appealing as possible and the fact that the excessive playing of video games is now officially recognised as a form of addiction provides a testament to their effectiveness (Gentile et al., 2017). Digital technologies have also enabled and enhanced the sophisticated 'nudging' of consumer behaviours. Whilst 'nudging' exists in the analogue world (in, e.g., the form of sweets by the supermarket check-out) it has risen to new levels of sophistication and effectiveness in our postdigital world. In particular, digital technology enables the tailored nudging of individuals based on harvesting and responding to data about their current preferences and predicted desires (as, e.g., in the case of Amazon product recommendations).

In addition to identifying potential ethical issues, a techno-ethical lens also proposes strategies for coping with these issues. First, a techno-ethical lens prompts us to focus on the specificities and technicalities of digital technologies. If ethics are embedded and materialised in the technicalities of product design, then ethicists must become well-versed in these technicalities if they wish to contribute to our ethical understandings of these products. Indeed, ethicists have a duty to make digital black boxes more transparent and to bring out their embedded and often hidden values, so that they can be opened up to broader democratic scrutiny. Second, a techno-ethical lens tells us that we are already too late to the game if we attempt to critically evaluate and govern digital technologies after they have entered general circulation. Instead, we must insist upon the ethical evaluation of a given technology at the design phase, before values and sets of assumptions have been cemented into the product. This practice has already been adopted in certain circumstances, with mechanisms such as 'Living Labs' (Følstad, 2008) encouraging multistakeholder participation at the early stages of product design; however issues of technological appropriateness and technological sovereignty remain.

Ethical Interfaces

Another potentially insightful area of ethical enquiry suggested by New Materialist approaches relates to the ethics of digital interfaces. As opposed to focusing on either the digital technologies themselves or their impacts on human users, a New Materialist approach might steer us towards an interest in the space between the machine and the user. Just as Deleuze and Guattari (1987) insist that wasps and orchids are locked together in a block of becoming and that it makes little sense to analyse their evolution as separate entities, so perhaps we should focus more ethical attention on the way digital technologies and human practices co-evolve. The ways in which humans and digital technologies connect are constantly evolving, from the typewriter keys and mice of computers, to the swipes and hand gestures of smartphones, to the speech recognition of Alexa and Siri, to the prompt-based interfaces of Large Language Models, such as ChatGPT and to the Brain Computer interfaces (BCIs) of Neuralink. Each method of connecting engenders a different type of interactivity and a different way in which we appear to the technology and the technology appears to us. Deleuze and Guattari (1987) have critiqued the face as the black hole of subjectivity and the white wall of signification; we might say the same about the interface between digital technologies and humans. As one speaks to Alexa, one learns how to ask the right types of questions in the right kind of ways in order for a successful interchange to occur. Alexa trains us how to speak and we train Alexa how to answer. Furthermore, by learning how to speak properly to Alexa we run the risk of forgetting how to speak properly to other humans. By paying attention to the relationality between humans and digital technologies we can gain deeper insights into the exchange and substitution of competencies that occur. For example, the more expert we become in using a certain software program or digital platform, the less we need to think for ourselves. It is at the interface that we can best understand the ways in which humans are re-skilled and de-skilled by digital technologies.

Digital Performativity

The final area of potentially fruitful ethical enquiry suggested by New Materialist approaches relates to the 'performativity' (or world making capacity) of digital technologies and digital modes of representation. The concept of 'performativity' refers to the ways in which representations do not merely mirror, reflect or represent material realities but rather they intervene in the world to move and shape it in certain ways (Mol, 2002). This concept originates in the work of linguists, such as Austin (1975) and Searle (1989), who coined the phrase 'speech acts' to refer to the ways in which language acts upon the socio-material world, for example, when one states 'I do' at a wedding ceremony this is akin to a 'leap of place' where socio-material-linguistic realities are transformed. Seen in this way, words can be far more than just descriptions. This notion also connects to the Deleuzian concept of 'order words' outlined in the previous section (Deleuze, 2004).

In the same way that New Materialist ideas provide novel insights into the material impacts of analogue representations, they can also shed light on the ways in which digital representations shape the world. Indeed, we would argue that the 'performative' or world making capacities of digital representations far exceed their analogue counterparts. This is primarily because digital forms of representation are more dynamic, reactive and mobile than their static analogue equivalents. For example, if we compare the performative capacity of a traditional motorway sign to that of a smart sign, connected to a smart motorway with an array of sensors collecting a constant stream of traffic information, then the differences should be clear. The former can only intervene in the world and order traffic flows in a fixed fashion, whereas the latter can issue a wide range of different instructions driven by insights delivered from real-time traffic information.

By using the lens of 'digital performativity' and attending to the world making capacity of digital technologies we can gain new insights into postdigital ethics. For example, when interrogating the arrays of digital sensors and digital signs that constitute smart cities, smart farms, smartphones and smart cars, we can ask what type of world are these digital technologies creating. With each novel coupling of digital sensor and digital response comes a new ethics of response-ability and we should ask what is being measured, what is the response, what is being optimised, in what ways and who made these decisions about what was and was not significant in this new postdigital world.

REFLECTION

In this chapter we have argued that our current ethical frameworks are ill-equipped to deal with our postdigital world and we have proposed alternative ethical approaches based on the ideas on New Materialist thinkers. If we accept that we inhabit a postdigital world, in which it is no longer possible to separate the digital from the non-digital, then we must also accept that this poses significant challenges to our current human-centred conceptual frameworks. In particular, ethical frameworks based on deontological, utilitarian or virtue-based approaches are all human-centric, and yet we live in a technological and digitised world in which humans, or at least humans acting alone, are no longer central to decision-making. This is not to say that we see no value in traditional ethical approaches or in attempts to extend and modify these approaches to interrogate the postdigital, however we do believe that these traditional approaches can be usefully supplemented with insights from New Materialism. Moreover, we believe that New Materialist thinkers, and in particular theorists such as Deleuze and Latour, have much to offer in both conceptualising our contemporary, digitally entangled lives and in unearthing the often hidden ethical dimensions of these entanglements.

By drawing on the insights of these thinkers we identified three potential lines of ethical enquiry. First, we proposed the notion of 'techno-ethics', which seeks to uncover the ways in which ethical values and power relations become embedded in technologies. Second, we discussed the notion of 'ethical interfaces' and the importance of attending to the space between the machine and the user. Third, we focused on 'digital performativity' (or the world making capacity) of digital technologies and digital modes of representation. Taken together all of these ethical lines of enquiry represent a modest, grounded and practical approach to understanding postdigital ethics. Rather than proposing grand over-arching theories of how we might value digital assets or providing frameworks to evaluate the broader societal impacts of digital culture, we have instead promoted a focus on the material details and ethical specificities of different digital technologies. For example, techno-ethics encourages ethicists to focus on the technicalities of digital technologies as part of the process of unearthing potentially hidden values and opening up technological and digital black boxes to broader democratic accountability. Likewise, focusing on ethical interfaces requires a practical focus on the precise nature and characteristics of a given interface coupled with a detailed empirical evaluation of specific human-digital interactions and how these evolve over time. Finally, focusing on digital performativity draws attention to the practical and material ways in which digital technologies shape our worlds. This is particularly apparent in the context of 'smart' technologies, such as smartphones, and 'smart' environments, such as smart cities or smart farms. Again, the focus here is on the detail and on specific empirical questions about how these smart environments operate, the types of digital sensors that are present, the types of information that is collected and the ways in which that information is used. All of these questions are potentially deeply political and deeply ethical as different decisions could have been made and things could have been otherwise.

CONCLUSIONS

As a final remark, and in keeping to the spirit of a modest approach to ethics, we would note that whilst New Materialism can provide very useful insights into postdigtial ethics, it does not provide all the answers. Indeed, John Reader believed that insights from New Materialism could be usefully combined with insights from Relational Christian Realism to gain a deeper understanding of contemporary ethical issues (Reader, 2017). Furthermore, whilst John embraced the worldly focus of New Materialism, he still believed that there was space for the divine in our ethical considerations.

REFERENCES

Austin, J. L. (1975). *How to do things with words.* Cambridge, Massachusetts: Harvard University Press.

Bennett, J. (2020). *Vibrant matter: A political ecology of things.* Durham, NC: Duke University Press.

Braidotti, R. (2013). *The posthuman.* Cambridge: Polity Press.

Bryant, L. (2011). *The democracy of objects.* Ann Arbor, Michigan: University of Michigan Library.

Clark, S. (2007). *The sun kings: The unexpected tragedy of Richard Carrington and the tale of how modern astronomy began.* Princeton and Oxford: Princeton University Press.

Coole, D., & Frost, S. (2010). *New materialisms: Ontology, agency, and politics.* Durham, NC: Duke University Press.

Cramer, F. (2015). What is 'post-digital'? In D. M. Berry & M. Dieter (Eds.), *Postdigital aesthetics: Art, computation and design* (pp. 12–26). London: Palgrave Macmillan. https://doi.org/10.1057/9781137437204_2

DeLanda, M. (2013). *Intensive science and virtual philosophy.* London: Bloomsbury Publishing.

Deleuze, G. (2004). *Logic of sense.* London: Bloomsbury Publishing.

Deleuze, G., & Guattari, F. (1987). *A thousand plateaus: Capitalism and schizophrenia.* Minneapolis, MN: University of Minnesota Press.

Dörner, K., & Edelman, D. (2015). *What 'digital' really means.* Boston, MA: McKinsey & Company.

Floridi, L. (1999). Information ethics: On the philosophical foundation of computer ethics. *Ethics and Information Technology,* 1(1), 33–52. https://doi.org/10.1023/A:1010018611096

Følstad, A. (2008). Living labs for innovation and development of information and communication technology: A literature review. *The Electronic Journal for Virtual Organizations and Networks (eJOV), 10,* 99–313.

Gentile, D. A., Bailey, K., Bavelier, D., Brockmyer, J. F., Cash, H., Coyne, S. M., & Young, K. (2017). Internet gaming disorder in children and adolescents. *Pediatrics,* 140(Supplement_2), S81–S85. https://doi.org/10.1542/peds.2016-1758H

Haraway, D. J. (2013). *When species meet.* (n.p.): University of Minnesota Press.

Ingold, T. (2021). *The perception of the environment: Essays on livelihood, dwelling and skill.* Abingdon, Oxon and New YorkRoutledge.

Jandrić, P., Knox, J., Besley, T., Ryberg, T., Suoranta, J., & Hayes, S. (2018). Postdigital science and education. *Educational Philosophy and Theory,* 50(10), 893–899. https://doi.org/10.1080/00131857.2018.1454000

Latour, B. (2004). *Politics of nature.* Cambridge, MA: Harvard University Press.

Latour, B. (2007). *Reassembling the social: An introduction to actor-network-theory.* Oxford: Oxford University Press.

McNeill, D. (2008, October 20). Virtual killer faces real jail after murder by mouse. *The Independent.* https://www.independent.co.uk/tech/virtual-killer-faces-real-jail-after-murder-by-mouse-972680.html

Meillassoux, Q. (2010). *After finitude: An essay on the necessity of contingency.* London: Bloomsbury Publishing.

Mol, A. (2002). *The body multiple: Ontology in medical practice.* Durham, NC: Duke University Press.

National Research Council. (2008). *Severe space weather events: Understanding societal and economic impacts: A workshop report.* Washington, DC: The National Academies Press. https://doi.org/10.17226/12507

Negroponte, N. (1998, January 12). Beyond digital. *Wired.* https://web.media.mit.edu/~nicholas/Wired/WIRED6-12.html

Oxford English Dictionary. (1989). *Oxford English dictionary.* Simpson, J. A., & Weiner, E. S. C. (Eds.), Oxford: Clarendon Press.

Reader, J. (2017). *Theology and new materialism: Spaces of faithful dissent.* Cham, Switzerland: Springer.

Reader, J., & Evans, A. (2019). *Ethics after new materialism: A modest undertaking.* London: The William Temple Foundation.

Rumbles, W. (2011). Theft in the digital: Can you steal virtual property? *Canterbury Law Review,* 17, 354.

Savin-Baden, M., & Reader, J. (Eds.). (2022). *Postdigital theologies: Technology, belief, and practice.* Cham, Switzerland: Springer Nature.

Searle, J. R. (1989). How performatives work. *Linguistics and Philosophy,* 12, 535–558. https://doi.org/10.1007/BF00627773

Stalder, F. (2018). *The digital condition.* Cambridge: Polity Press.

Stengers, I. (2018). *Another science is possible: A manifesto for slow science.* Cambridge: Polity Press.

Stiegler, B. (1998). *Technics and time 1: The fault of epimetheus.* Stanford, CA: Stanford University Press.

3 Searching for the Good Life
Boundary Crossing, Co-Existence and Conviviality

Mark Coeckelbergh and John Reader

INTRODUCTION

What happens when a theologian and a philosopher talk about technology and relationality?

ABOUT THE CONVERSATION

This dialogue between Mark Coeckelbergh and John Reader took place online in April 2023.

AI ETHICS FOR THE PEOPLE

John Reader (JR): In *AI Ethics* (Coeckelbergh 2020: 168–177) you talk about the need for a bottom-up approach in contrast to applied ethics which tends to be top-down and abstract. You go on to say that everyday ethics may not be a matter of fully articulate reasoning as we need to recognise that the way we respond to issues is always embedded in a 'form of life' (173). This implies that there are limits of a deliberative approach and while it is necessary to have methods and procedures, these are not sufficient for a full engagement as 'ethics does not work like a machine' (173). I feel this draws on a very interesting understanding of what it is to be human and how we function in practice. Can you say how this is grounded in practice and in philosophical sources?

Mark Coeckelbergh (MC): Abstraction can be useful in ethics as in other domains, and philosophers tend to be good at this. However, we sometimes forget that ethics is meant for people, who are embedded in practices and who have lives in which they are confronted with concrete situations and contexts. For this understanding of ethics, I'm very much indebted to

 DOI: 10.1201/9781003497950-4

John Dewey's pragmatism, which is anti-foundationalist and sees ethics in situated terms. Interestingly, this kind of ethics also makes room for improvisation and experiment. Often rules and principles are not enough to deal with an ethical problem; then we have to use our moral imagination. Steven Fesmire has written an interesting book on this (Fesmire 2003) and I also used this kind of thinking in my book, *Imagination and Principles: An Essay on the Role of Imagination in Moral Reasoning* (Coeckelbergh 2017).

Another source is Wittgenstein, in particular the *Philosophical Investigations* (1953/2009). 'Form of life' is his term for the background of everyday life that gives meaning to what we do and that structures what we do. It is a kind of background grammar. Wittgenstein also talks about language games. What we do with language cannot just rely on rules but depends on an often-inexplicit background of ways of doing things in a culture. I have used the same thinking for understanding how we perform with technology: the meaning of our engagements with technology depends on such a form of life (Coeckelbergh 2018). This is also interesting for doing philosophy of technology in an intercultural way: we should ask how different forms of life impact how we use technology and vice versa.

JR: Can you expand a little on 'forms of life' and embedding? What might these mean in practice?

MC: Bottom-up approaches are also helpful in philosophy of technology because they encourage us to listen to what developers of technology have to say on these issues. And they recommend listening to those who are potentially affected by technology: stakeholders.

JR: What kind of stakeholders do we need? How do we involve so-called ordinary people, apart from the academy?

MC: If there is a nuclear power plant you ask the people who live in that area. If you develop AI that has potentially billions of users, that's more difficult. But social scientists have methods to create groups of representative citizens that can participate in more democratic forms of decision making. For Dewey, ethics was also about democracy: about doing things together, about community, about experimenting together as a society.

JR: We often think of AI as something 'out there', but as with globalisation and consumerism, to a greater or lesser extent, we are part of this, aren't we? We make use of AI and what it produces, sometimes without knowing the processes and their implications. How do we encourage ethical responses to AI from a wide range of stakeholders, when AI is already part of our lives and is often thought of as contributing to our modern lifestyle and lifestyle choices?

MC: That's right, AI is already part of our lives. People often blame the developers of technology, especially Big Tech. And there is truth in that: they have a very important responsibility, and they need to be regulated and encouraged and forced to take up that responsibility. But as users of technology, we are also responsible. I have argued that we are part of the process. That gives us also responsibility for the technology. If we organise the development of technology in a more participative and democratic way, then we can also exercise the responsibility.

But we can also relate to the existing technologies in a more critical way. We should stop seeing ourselves only as victims of those who make the technology. We can resist, and we can 'hack' the technology. Not all of us have a technical background, but we can use the technology in a different way than it's meant, if that helps us to live more meaningful lives. Let's be creative, let's improvise, let's experiment.

Of course, this is not only an individual issue; we should also question and change the system. If we don't do that, it's very difficult for individuals to make a change.

JR: In *AI Ethics* (Coeckelbergh 2020: 179) you talk about the possibility of the idea of a more diverse and holistic kind of *Bildung* or narrative that is more radically interdisciplinary and pluralistic with regard to methods and approaches and its topics. Assuming this means something like cultural framing or conceptual context, how do you see religion or religions featuring in this and contributing to a wider narrative? I am aware that there are cultural and political differences in approaches to the public role of religion between the UK and other European nations …

MC: Religions are part of human culture, of course, and depending on the context they can play a role in the public sphere and in education. Which role is a political question? In a democracy, a separation between religious and political authorities is needed. That being said, in a secular education that aims to be pluralistic it might be a good idea that people learn about various religious traditions and worldviews. This can help to foster tolerance, important in a liberal-democratic society. It may also help people in their search for meaning.

The current educational systems in the West are too focused on academic skills and neglect the search for the good life and the need for making sense of the world. We need more philosophy in education, and giving people more knowledge about various religions can be part of that.

CROSSING BOUNDARIES

JR: We both seem intent on crossing boundaries and your response does so in really important ways, but also ones about which I have reservations. In order to make sense of those I need to explain more of my own position. As both a practitioner and also engaged with more theoretical debates, I have found myself crossing boundaries beyond the church but also in terms of other disciplines which help me analyse the situations I encounter. With the first I have worked with community groups and non-religious organisations as we share commitments to issues such as the environment, education, and housing. I have described this as 'blurred encounters' (Baker and Reader 2009) and tried to offer a rationale for this approach. I particularly like what Derrida (1991; see also Reader 2005; Reader et al. 2020) said about being eaten well. Going down this route, it is inevitable that one becomes to some degree appropriated by the other activity or discipline, and rather than imagining one can avoid 'being eaten', the sensible objective is to aim for being eaten well.

I cross the boundary between theology and philosophy in particular but also with other disciplines such as sociology and psychology as I try to understand complex contexts and responses to them. I also work with the William Temple Foundation which has a long history of social and political engagement from a Christian UK perspective, and this gives a different approach to some of the areas you articulate in that last response.

Placing religions within a cultural context and viewing them as sources of ethical values and relevant to a wider educational project is fair enough on one level but may well be challenged by religions themselves. We would probably agree that both 'culture' and 'religion' are contested concepts which cover a wide variety of approaches and self-understandings. Both categories could be disputed, especially in this pluralistic situation to which you refer.

Leaving that to one side however, there are differences between the role of religion in public life in the UK and other European countries which I need to register. Obvious ones are that the Monarch is the Head of the Church of England, so when I take up my new post, I will swear allegiance to King Charles and his successors as well as to the church hierarchy. Whether or not one agrees with this, and whether or not one thinks it makes any real difference, it means that at the moment Bishops (some of them) sit in the House of Lords, there are many Church of England schools, and there is a civic role for the established church in England. Hence the separation between church and state to which you refer is more complex, entangled and blurred in my context.

Other denominations and other faiths often find this frustrating and difficult to negotiate, but it can also mean that there is a faith representation at both local and national political level and that is seen as a positive advantage. At the church school where I was heavily involved there were Muslim families who preferred their children to attend a faith school (albeit Christian) rather than a non-faith school. There are many examples of good interfaith working at local level in urban settings of which the William Temple Foundation could provide examples. My colleagues talk about 'spiritual capital', for instance, and the wider resources of faith communities as they engage in local action, crossing those religious boundaries.

These would be good examples of 'tolerance' which you mention, although I am aware that even that term is questioned as being too 'soft' and not acknowledging the real differences between the different faiths. It is Derrida (in Borradori 2003) again I think who challenges the concept of tolerance. The relationships need to go beyond 'mere tolerance' to identify genuine differences and disagreements. I prefer the concept of hospitality which Derrida uses of course drawn from Levinas and is then used by theologians such as Kearney and Keller.

I suppose that what concerns me about what you have said is that it may not fully take into account the self-understandings of the specific faiths and their communities. Going back to Derrida's (1991; see also Reader 2005; Reader et al. 2020) idea of being eaten well, such an approach has to take into account questions of identity and integrity when the boundaries are crossed and engagements both with other faiths and other disciplines take place. What I and others are keen to tease out is which particular beliefs and practices either inhibit or enable creative and positive 'blurred encounters'. Ideas of hierarchy, the role of the human in relation to creation or the non-human generally and of transcendence of course are each potentially inhibiting ones when it comes to the environment and also the digital.

That is a very long way of saying that you and I share concerns about both the environment and the digital, plus a deep engagement with particular philosophical traditions, but what I hope our discussion will enable is an exploration of those inhibiting and enabling factors. What are the ideas that you promote that make common cause with a faith-based approach that I would support? That is why I would like you to say more about what you understand by 'the good life'; the 'search for meaning' and indeed 'making sense of the world' in *Digital Technologies, Temporality, and the Politics of Co-Existence* (Coeckelbergh 2023). I sense from what you say in other places (Coeckelbergh 2022a: 150) that you are arguing for new understandings of the concepts and values of: freedom, equality, justice, democracy, power, human-centred politics. Also you question the roles of expertise, rationality and emotions in politics, and I think these could be at the heart of our discussion.

Just as you are 'pushing the boundaries' from within your discipline, so I believe that I (and others) are pushing the boundaries from within our disciplines in response to the ecological crises and the dominance of the digital. How can we support and resource each other in that task? I am keen to develop a new conceptual framework which will enable critical engagements with the concerns that we share. Can you say more about the new concepts that you want to develop?

MC: When it comes to institutional politics I insist on a liberal-philosophical position, which means in this case that religion and politics need to be separated and that there needs to be tolerance. I think the way things are set up in the UK is problematic from this point of view. One can have other channels to have conversations. But intellectually speaking, tolerance is of course not enough; it can only be a minimum. Intellectually, we need to look for the maximum. Here, and as you suggest, real engagement is needed with the views of others, including between non-religious and religious people, and between different faiths. Even going beyond hospitality perhaps, because the guest remains a stranger whereas in a deeper existential sense we are all strangers, but hospitality would already get us a long way.

In any case, the deeper engagement and the interdisciplinary boundary crossing you mention are much needed today when we are faced with the ecological crisis and the ways digital technologies are transforming our culture and society. Here I see commonalities between secular and religious relational approaches that could help us to overcome the limited ways we now deal with our problems. Most ancient religions and world-views, not only the monotheistic ones but also so-called nature religions and indigenous views, help us to think beyond the human as an individual. They thus present resources for more relational thinking.

For this transformation, ethically and politically speaking, it is less important if one calls it religion or not. The main thing is that people move on to a more relational way of thinking and find each other under the umbrella of a relational project that can tackle the current global problems. As you know 'religion' means of course *re-ligare*, reconnect, relate again. In that sense, we need a more religious kind of thinking, a thinking that relates and reconnects.

I'm not against including emotions in politics, also not when we're talking about liberal-democratic politics. Emotions can of course be dangerous, but they can also help us to sense what is important. They can help us in a search for the good life and the common good. I would also like to mention the term 'co-existence'. In my latest book, *Digital Technologies, Temporality, and the Politics of Co-Existence* (Coeckelbergh 2023), I think about existence and co-existence in times of AI, COVID-19 and climate change. I talk about the need for a new kind of synchronisation. The point is that politics is often thought of as finding a commonplace.

That's part of what we need to do. However, we also need to find a common time. One problem for co-existence today is that we no longer share a common time, except the time that capitalism gives us. The challenge is then to find a new form of co-existence that has a different kind of 'good time'. The good life is not only about good places but also about good times. In the past religions provided a way to synchronise, to bring us together in the same places and to create a common time. The challenge today, in a secular or pluralistic environment, is how to find common time now. Philosophical and theological traditions can help us with this relational project.

JR: Your comment about the possibility of finding a common time sparked a response to which you then replied as follows: this is key for me in what you write: "Hence my question as to whether there can be a 'digital chora' or time/moment when the unexpected and even unwelcome breaks through and sparks off deeper reflection and response".

At the time I was writing my *Theology and New Materialism: Spaces of Faithful Dissent* (Reader 2017) and reflecting on the work of Stiegler and Derrida from philosophy and the theologians Keller and Kearney. I was also speculating on whether there could be both spaces and times for what I called faithful dissent or opportunities for resistance to the dominant and damaging human impacts upon both human and non-human worlds. It seems clear that their concern was focused on time and the means by which digital technology makes the future present in ways that are not entirely subject to human control, at least by those on the receiving end of the process.

Spaces of faithful dissent are not limited to physical or even geographical locations but must also bring time into the picture. Spaces mean opportunities, moments when alternatives can emerge or be imagined as well as the more obvious locations where this might occur. Are there alternative times available in the present, something like the chora which Keller and Kearney talk about and even the 'beyond in the midst' which I used (Reader 2017: 48) with reference to Bonhoeffer (1997)? Can 'the beyond' refer to time as well as space? The objective then is to identify possible sources which might begin to address that question. Perhaps you could say more about the direction in which your reflections upon time have taken this research.

MC: Yes, it's important to ask how digital technologies make the future present. This is not only a question of control but also about the precise quality and nature of the experience of the future and the ways this making-present of the future also shapes our present actions – and hence the future. For example, a prediction by AI might lead to me taking a different action and in that way shape the present and the future. This is about AI controlling us, but it's even more about how the technology shapes what we think, do and think of ourselves. Even if we retain some control or even if we can resist, there is nevertheless an influence. We are forced to respond so to speak. Resistance is one kind of response.

That resistance is about spaces and times, yes, places and times when and where alternatives can be imagined and can emerge. Any 'beyond' is usually imaged in terms of space. A different place. Or a non-place and 'elsewhere' place. A utopia. However, we might also imagine a 'beyond' in terms of time. A different time. A non-time perhaps. I guess theology offers ways to think about this.

Much secular thinking about better times and alternative times, from Marx to transhumanism, seems to have similarities with theological thinking. Consider thinking about 'end times', for example. I have an article, in a theology volume edited by a German Catholic philosopher and theologian Benedikt Paul Göcke, titled 'Transcendence Machines: Transhumanism and Its Technical-Religious Sources' (Coeckelbergh 2018). It's about how technology becomes an instrument for trying to reach transcendence. Transhumanism is a secular version of that. It looks for a technological 'beyond'.

JR: There are emerging resonances between your approach to the question of co-existence and alternative experiences or performances of time and what I see as religious understandings of time. I think we agree that the search for common spaces is increasingly hampered as what we call the public or civic sphere is hollowed out and populated instead by echo chambers. I like the phrases you use to point towards alternatives. So we need to develop political ecologies of time; a relational time of immanence and that there should be a multitude of temporalities rather than dominant, linear or totalising time (Coeckelbergh 2023: 66). These lead to your synchronicities of resistance as we search for different ways of making meaning together which challenge what I would call the enclosures of capitalism. Then there is the striving to understand time as beyond the human with an awareness of deep time as recounted for instance in Thomas Halliday's *Otherlands: A Journey Through* Earth's Extinct Worlds (2023) which tracks back as far as 550 million years ago and the earliest emergence of life on this planet. To see time in this perspective is to place the human itself in question.

Within the Christian tradition there are different understandings of time. Chronos or clock time is only one aspect of this as there is also Kairos meaning the right time, the moment at which something new breaks in or which sparks transformative activity. This was illustrated in South Africa for instance when apartheid was broken apart and new freedoms emerged. There is also cyclical time; the repetition which one experiences in the liturgical calendar moving through the seasons from Easter through Advent, Christmas and Lent. This provides a different sort of continuity and stability.

As a jazz fan I am also reminded of the ground-breaking work of Miles Davis who was the first to use polyrhythms and polytonalities in order to disrupt the normal timings of the music and create something new in albums such as *In a Silent Way* (1969a) and *Bitches Brew* (1969b). Yet one could argue that the most important aspect of the music was always the spaces or the silences in the phrasing, particularly of his own playing. The sound relies on the silences or gaps in order to create the whole. This is what concerns me about the digital which, as I have argued elsewhere (Reader 2023), presents us with a full or pure presence which doesn't allow for the gaps and absences which are an essential part of our experience of both space and time. The metaverse would seem an obvious example of this full presence or enclosure.

Where are the times and spaces for what Catherine Keller (2021; see also Keller and Jandrić 2022) calls dreamreading and what Bernard Stiegler (2019: Chapter 7) calls intermittances? Some of my theological colleagues believe that the Trinity provides the framework for a positive response to the digital by constructing the 'hyperdigital' subsuming the technology in a Christianised Hegelian *Aufhebung*, but they ignore what is called *perichoresis*, or the Divine Dance which allows space (and time) for alternatives and the unexpected to break through and disrupt what risks becoming yet another enclosure (Rohr 2016). Then, as you say, there is the subject of the 'end times' which may well mean the end of the human but not the end of the planet (and beyond). How do we learn to co-exist in the light of the possibility that the human will either cease or be so transformed as to be unrecognisable?

THE TIME OF BREATHING

JR: This is where we turn to the subject of the environment, so let's now explore possible resonances in this area. How does your emphasis upon the relational and the search for a good life relate to the challenge of climate change, for instance?

MC: These are very interesting alternative understandings of time: alternative to the time of science, the time of social media, the time of capitalism. And we should indeed be avoiding a technologically created situation in which there is a totalizing presence, a music without silences, the end of dance. We need disruptions of time.

The current situation regarding environmental matters is sometimes called the Anthropocene. The Anthropocene is the time of the human, the time when humans have so much influence on the planet that even the climate changes. It is a kind of hyper-agency. It also becomes a totalising kind of time, in the sense that everything is sucked into the time of the human. We are forced into that order, but also other beings are forced and ordered. In order to get out of that, in order to disrupt, in order to create a different kind of music, we need a more relational kind of thinking and a notion of co-existence that is more inclusive.

Relational thinking means that we should act and think in a way that always links the human to the non-human, because we are nothing without the natural environment, without all the relevant ecologies and terrestrial environments. In contrast to what hyper-modern existentialists like Sartre thought, our existence is not entirely up to us, it is also to some extent given. What we are and who we are is not entirely a matter of design.

That can be interpreted not only religiously but also ecologically. We have technology, but ultimately, we have no choice when it comes to life: our environment and other beings give us constraints. You can design whatever you want, you can use a lot of technology, but there will be limits. Limits to what you can be as a human being, limits to what you can become as a person, limits to what you can do given that you are an embodied being that is part of a wider ecology. Such ideas have been around for a while. Think of deep ecology for example. However, we keep pushing the boundaries in a modern way. Pushing boundaries may well be part of what it is to be human, but there are limits to that. We are natural, social and (if you add religion) spiritual beings; we cannot change into something or someone completely different.

The good life, then, is not about individual well-being as such but is always a question of co-existence and conviviality, of living together. I also think of Ivan Illich here. Any politics should be an environmental and convivial kind of politics, it should not be about individual interests but about the question of how to live together and how to create a good kind of interdependence, given that we are relational beings. Aristotle called that 'political animals'. It is also a more inclusive kind of politics: other beings also matter. Even after so many decades of environmental movement, animal rights, etc., we still do politics as if we are the only inhabitants of the earth. It's time to change that.

JR: It feels as though we are moving towards a crescendo of agreement as I share with you the search for an approach which acknowledges the co-existence of the human and the non-human. I have found Latour's work so helpful in this regard as also some of the ideas emerging from New Materialism which talks about assemblages and distributed agency. But I am also reminded again of one of my favourite theologians Catherine Keller in her *Political Theology of the Earth: Our Planetary Emergency and the Struggle for a* New Public (2018).

Her starting point is that time itself seems to be running out which faces Christians with the immediate issue of whether or not we believe in some predetermined outcome for creation. She interprets St. Paul's teaching on the subject as being about 'the now time' (Keller 2018: 2). This does not mean the end of the world itself but the end of a particular human construction of the world. Somewhat as with 'death of God' debates, the question is that of which God and which world. Running through the text is a commitment to apophatic entanglement which she describes in greater detail in *Cloud of the Impossible: Negative Theology and Planetary Entanglement* (Keller 2014). The inescapable question is that of hope in the face of the coming crisis and what this might mean given the reformulations of both politics and theology.

Keller's chapter (Keller 2018: Chapter 1) on the political takes us into the works of Mouffe and Schmitt. Keller suggests that our chance, if we have one, lies in the indeterminate, and helpfully defines the political as 'collective assemblage across critical difference' (Keller 2018: 33). In other words, we must avoid the trap of a false unity or consensus and accept that differences even within radical approaches are acceptable and inevitable. The task, as those of us who read Latour would say, is to understand the human and the non-human in connection and collaboration, and this is where the discourse of assemblages is so important. All echoes of the state of exception, or the sovereign empire, have to be abandoned along with visions of a secure future, and instead we need to understand that we are dealing with energy, dynamic materiality, flux, movement and uncertainty (67). Is this the basis for shared experience and a new public space (and time) that appropriately and effectively provides a base for tackling the climate crisis?

Discussions of the Anthropocene shade into the Capitalocene (Keller 2018: 82), Haraway's Chthulucene and into the Ecocene (Keller 2018: 91), including Pope Francis's call for an integral ecology. The element which both Keller and I believe is necessary along with an emphasis upon the relational is an appreciation of the apophatic – that which remains beyond articulation and places the human in a wider spiritual context, hence 'the cloud of unknowing'. Just one quote will hopefully serve to illustrate this.

> The apophatic unknowing cultivates hospitality to shared uncertainty. Its practice can host in its very darkness collective indeterminacies, whether unspeakable in horror, in precarity, or in wonder. As a minimal form of apophatic practice, the moment of silent breathing together (con-spiratio) already begins to gather a public across difference.
>
> (Keller 2018: 164)

Here there are echoes of the search for alternative practices of being together and co-existence, the silent music or spaces of a different time which is so much more than just the human.

Having said that, I am reminded of another Miles Davis' album *Kind of* Blue (1959), purportedly one of the best of all time, and for me that sets a mood which predominates my feelings about the future. I love the blues as conveying senses of loss, longing and even lament. Perhaps it is a function of age that one looks back to the baseline of better times (which they never were of course) rather than forward with optimism. With both the digital and the environmental we tread a thin line between hope and despair, and I note that many books on these subjects close on an optimistic and hopeful note. Better for selling books I suppose than being miserable and downbeat.

I also rely on Stiegler's (2015) concept of the pharmakon, taken from Derrida who took it from Plato, with the digital being both poison and remedy and sometimes both at the same time. In your book, *Self-Improvement* (Coeckelbergh 2022b: 107), you close on a basically upbeat note suggesting that technologies can be part of the solution as well as of the problem. Technologies can help us towards a different kind of self-knowledge; one that knows its limits; delivering a more sustainable and deeper kind of self-development. These can help us understand ourselves in a relational way as partners in personal but also collective processes of self-improvement. As you said earlier, technologies are embedded in forms of life and part of larger social and cultural wholes.

The other side of the argument though is that we face a raft of growing dangers such as the threat of the nuclear related not only to Ukraine but also a stand-off between China and the US over Taiwan. Six of the nine planetary boundaries including climate change and biodiversity have already been crossed. There may be yet more pandemics plus we are presented with right-wing authoritarian regimes who deploy the digital to control and enclose. For a really cheerful read try Nouriel Roubini's *MegaThreats: Ten Dangerous Trends That Imperil Our Future, And How to* Survive Them (2022) although even he attempts to conclude on a positive note. So my final question is of how well-founded is your optimism. Are we going to rock and roll into a brighter future or will be singing the blues together, and what will make the difference between those scenarios?

MC: I agree with you that the end of a particular human construction of the world is in sight, or perhaps is already happening and to some extent has already happened. After the death of God there is the death of the Human in the sense of the end of anthropocentrism. We can also no longer appeal to a kind of unity that was exclusive and oppressing. Nevertheless, exactly in these times, I think cooperation and a good kind of unity, a good kind of relationality are more needed than ever. A co-existence that accepts uncertainty and that gathers and cooperates in the face of it and engaging with it. To do that in a critical way, it is great to search for alternative spaces and times. Religions can help with that search, next to other approaches.

Hope and despair belong together. They are two sides of the same coin. It's ok to sing the blues. Then the next step is making a different kind of music. Technology as pharmakon can help, at least if it is transformed and embedded in a more relational, collective and collecting project. I share your concerns about the future. However, I think part of the problem is that we think too dualistically about the future. It's either bright or disastrous. We are optimistic or pessimistic. Maybe to get out of that *cul-de-sac* we need to focus on transforming the present, on creating good times – to use a term I use in my book. Not just on an individual level, of course. The point is to do it in a relational, holistic way, in a way that influences the world.

But I'm not naïve about politics. We need to also do it in ways that use and interact with power, including criticising how powerful actors currently shape and narrate the technological present and future in ways that lead to colossal problems. After the blues we need resistance and transformation. Rock, if you like. Energy is needed. I sense that such a change is already happening.

But experiencing the silence of the soul and creating and listening to new sounds that show us new, other possibilities can also be part of that process of change. Maybe this is needed to really, or more deeply, transform. From blues and jazz, we can learn that improvisation is also about responding to others. In a sense you never play alone. You respond to patterns of the past and you respond to what others do – even if they are not physically present. In the mentioned book on pragmatist ethics, Steven Fesmire (2003) talks about how jazz musicians tune and respond to others. It's a relational kind of activity. However, it's not just about humans. In our improvisations of the good life, we have to respond to what's going on in the world.

The breathing together that you mention can also help the change. Breathing is a good metaphor: it is relational *par excellence*. It is deeply environmental. It (re-)connects us with others and with the world. Breathing is never just about humans and never just about me. Breathing participates in the flux of the world and in the rhythm of life itself, and in that sense receives and at the same time gives. It contributes to change, it *is* change. Breathing is time itself that relates and circulates. We see time usually as an arrow that shoots in one direction, towards the future. However, what about understanding time as a kind of breathing? And good times and good co-existence as a good kind of breathing together? Whereas hope and despair rip us apart by stretching us into the future, breathing brings us to the present. Present as 'now' and present as 'gift' and 'sharing'. Air cannot be kept. It needs to be received, given and shared. That's what good times are all about.

REFERENCES

Baker, C., James, T., & Reader, J. (2015). *A Philosophy of Christian Materialism: Entangled Fidelities and the Public Good*. Farnham: Ashgate.

Baker, C. R., & Reader, J. (Eds.). (2009). *Entering the New Theological Space: Blurred Encounters of Faith, Politics and Community*. London: Routledge. https://doi.org/10.4324/9781315579863.

Bonhoeffer, D. (1997). *Letters and Papers from Prison*. Chicago, IL: Touchstone.

Borradori, G. (2003). *Philosophy in a Time of Terror: Dialogues with Jurgen Habermas and Jacques Derrida*. Chicago, IL: The University of Chicago Press.

Coeckelbergh, M. (2017). *Imagination and Principles: An Essay on the Role of Imagination in Moral Reasoning.* London: Palgrave Macmillan. https://doi.org/10.1057/9780230589803.
Coeckelbergh, M. (2018). Transzendenzmaschinen: Der Transhumanismus und seine religiösen Quellen. In B. P. Göcke (Ed.), *Designobjekt Mensch: Die Agenda des Transhumanismus auf dem Prüfstand* (pp. 81–93). Freiburg im Breisgau: Herder.
Coeckelbergh, M. (2020). *AI Ethics.* Cambridge, MA: The MIT Press.
Coeckelbergh, M. (2022a). *The Political Philosophy of AI.* Cambridge: Polity.
Coeckelbergh, M. (2022b). *Self-Improvement.* New York: Columbia University Press.
Coeckelbergh, M. (2023). *Digital Technologies, Temporality, and the Politics of Co-Existence.* Cham: Palgrave Macmillan. https://doi.org/10.1007/978-3-031-17982-2.
Davis, M. (1959). *Kind of Blue* [Record]. New York: CBS.
Davis, M. (1969a). *In a Silent Way* [Record]. New York: CBS.
Davis, M. (1969b). *Bitches Brew* [Record]. New York: CBS.
Derrida, J. (1991). "Eating Well", or the Calculation of the Subject: An interview with Jacques Derrida. In E. Cadava, P. Connor, & J.-L. Nancy (Eds.), *Who Comes After the Subject?* (pp. 96–119). New York and London: Routledge.
Fesmire, S. (2003). *John Dewey and Moral Imagination: Pragmatism in Ethics.* Bloomington, IN: Indiana University Press.
Halliday, T. (2023). *Otherlands: A Journey Through Earth's Extinct Worlds.* New York: Random House.
Keller, C. (2014). *Cloud of the Impossible: Negative Theology and Planetary Entanglement.* New York: Columbia University Press.
Keller, C. (2018). *Political Theology of the Earth: Our Planetary Emergency and the Struggle for a New Public.* New York: Columbia University Press.
Keller, C. (2021). *Facing Apocalypse: Climate, Democracy, and Other Last Chances.* Maryknoll, NY: Orbis Books.
Keller, C., & Jandrić, P. (2022). Process Theology Against Global Capitalism: Towards an Ecological Civilization. In M. Savin-Baden & J. Reader (Eds.), *Postdigital Theologies: Technology, Belief, and Practice* (pp. 21–37). Cham: Springer. https://doi.org/10.1007/978-3-031-09405-7_2.
Reader, J. (2005). *Blurred Encounters: A Reasoned Practice of Faith.* Vale of Glamorgan: Aureus Publishing.
Reader, J. (2017). *Theology and New Materialism: Spaces of Faithful Dissent.* Basingstoke, UK: Palgrave Macmillan. https://doi.org/10.1007/978-3-319-54511-0.
Reader, J. (2023). Postdigital Research and Human Agency. In P. Jandrić, A. MacKenzie, & J. Knox (Eds.), *Postdigital Research: Genealogies, Challenges, and Future Perspectives.* Cham: Springer. pp. 213–230. https://doi.org/10.1007/978-3-031-31299-1_12.
Reader, J., Jandrić, P., Peters, M. A., Barnett, R., Garbowski, M., Lipińska, V., Rider, S., Bhatt, I., Clarke, A., Hashemi, M., Bevan, A., Trozzo, E., Mackenzie, A., Aldern, J. J., Matias, C. E., Stewart, G. T., Mika, C., McLaren, P., Fawns, T., Knox, J., Savin-Baden, M., Jackson, L., Hood, N., Tesar, M., Fuller, S., & Baker, C. (2020). Enchantment – Disenchantment – Re-Enchantment: Postdigital Relationships Between Science, Philosophy, and Religion. *Postdigital Science and Education,* 3(3), 934–965. https://doi.org/10.1007/s42438-020-00133-4.
Rohr, R. (2016). *The Divine Dance.* London: SPCK.
Roubini, N. (2022). *MegaThreats: Ten Dangerous Trends That Imperil Our Future, and How to Survive Them.* London: John Murray Publishers.
Stiegler, B. (2015). *What Makes Life Worth Living: On Pharmacology.* Cambridge, UK: Polity.
Stiegler, B. (2019). *The Age of Disruption: Technology and Madness in Computational Capitalism.* Cambridge: Polity Press.
Wittgenstein, L. (1953/2009). *Philosophische untersuchungen/Philosophical Investigations.* Revised 4th ed. Trans. G. E. M. Anscombe, P. M. S. Hacker, & J. Schulte. Malden, MA: Wiley.

Part II

Practical Theology and Ethics

4 Postdigital Cloud Prayer

Eric Trozzo

INTRODUCTION

What contribution might prayer make to postdigital Christian theology, spirituality and ethics? This question assumes that Christian prayer and postdigital theory are in fact compatible, which may not be an obvious assumption. Spirituality is often viewed as an internal discipline and prayer as a personal conversation with God. Taken in this vein, prayer would seem to have little to do with concerns of technology or theoretical frameworks. Such forms of piety do not seem to have much consonance with postdigital thought. Looking more closely at postdigital theory and other approaches to prayer, however, I suggest that a greater resonance can be found and Christian prayer can be seen to contribute to postdigital concerns.

As there is no single agreed-upon definition of what constitutes the 'postdigital', I will position my understanding by identifying three key characteristics of postdigital thought that are central to my thinking and relevant to considering spirituality from a Christian perspective.

(1) The postdigital rejects a separation between the digital and the non-digital. The two are deeply and increasingly integrated into one another. The postdigital views digital technologies as embedded within a larger field of material, social, economic and political concerns (Fawns et al., 2023).
(2) The experience of a self or subjectivity cannot be reduced to the limits of physical existence. One's online experiences and encounters are also a real aspect of recognising oneself as having subjectivity (Radde-Antweiler, 2022).
(3) Postdigital thought specifically addresses global challenges faced by humanity, seeking justice and liberation (McLaren and Jandrić, 2020, p. 255).

A common thread in these three characteristics is a rejection of separation between binary notions. Distinctions digital/non-digital, online/offline self and theory/activism are not separations; the sides of the divide are implicated in one another. From these three, for postdigital thought generally, my argument in this chapter is to add a religious one: rejecting a division between spirituality and engagement.

Postdigital prayer, then, would need to integrate these four seeming divides. The prayer would need to allow for a sense of self that includes the body yet extends beyond it, including virtual and online aspects in its subjectivity. The prayer would also need to recognise a role for the technological and digital within its understanding of connection with the divine. The prayer would further need to enable ethical

DOI: 10.1201/9781003497950-6

action on issues of justice and liberation, giving a spiritual and religious grounding to its activism.

In this chapter, I argue that within the Christian tradition it is contemplative prayer that is best suited to be a model of prayer in a postdigital spirituality. In particular, the apophatic tradition as represented through *The Cloud of Unknowing* is a fertile source for inspiring postdigital prayer. This medieval text cannot be directly applied, however. Rather, its themes can open new paths for contemplative postdigital prayer, just as it has inspired contemporary spiritual practices such as centring prayer and contemporary academic theological considerations of ethical concerns. To adapt it to the postdigital situation, the relationship of subjectivity to technology needs to be rethought in a postdigital manner. To that end, I propose drawing on Guattari's concept of the 'machinic unconscious' to reframe subjectivity that incorporates the technological.

THEOLOGY AND PRAYER IN THE CLOUD TRADITION

The Cloud of Unknowing and Contemplative Prayer

The Cloud of Unknowing is an anonymously written 14th-century British Christian devotional writing. It draws on the apophatic and mystical strands of Christian thought (Clarke, 2019), while primarily being a guide for a meditative form of prayer within a monastic context. The term 'cloud of unknowing' dates from Dionysius the Areopagite in the 6th or 7th century, who used it to describe the cloud over Mt. Sinai when Moses received the tablets of the commandments in Exodus 24. It symbolises the apophatic tradition of 'negative' theology that looks beyond the capacity of words to engage the ineffability of the divine. The writing has had enduring appeal, influencing both academic theology and spiritual practices.

The *Cloud* writer lays out a meditative practice aimed at a mystical sense of union with God. To do so, aspects of the sense of self must be released so that a sense of nothingness can be encountered. It is in this nothingness that the presence of God is met. The author clarifies that the self that is dealt with in spiritual writings is the spirit rather than the physical body (Wolters, 1978, p. 137). This is not a renunciation of the body but a matter of emphasis on matters of spiritual concern relating to the divine. The author identifies three major aspects of the soul and two minor ones. Major aspects are mind, intellect and will, while the minor ones are imagination and sensuality (Wolters, 1978, p. 137). The mind does little in itself, but rather holds the other faculties. Imagination or the ability to picture things and sensuality or the connection to bodily reactions are difficult to control and not central to the *Cloud*'s methodology. The intellect and the will are the central concerns of this spiritual practice.

The intellect is used to distinguish good from evil and make sense of the world. Its ability to do this, however, is corrupted by sin (Wolters, 1978, p. 138). The intellect, the *Cloud* author holds, cannot handle an encounter with God. Rather, it can only perceive truths about God (Meninger, 1996, p. 6). The recognition of the impossibility of thinking of God within God's own being is the entry into the unknowingness of mystical awareness that the metaphor of the 'cloud of unknowing' represents.

God is beyond the capacity of human thought. God's kindness or the value of the divine can be contemplated, but not God in God's own being. The desire to use the intellect to comprehend God must then be released. 'Therefore I will leave on one side everything I can think, and choose for my love that thing which I cannot think', the writer explains (Wolters, 1978, p. 68). This release is explained as a 'cloud of forgetting' that must cover one's thoughts in order to approach the cloud of unknowing.

Rather than the intellect, it is the will that can seek union with the divine and receive its truth (Meninger, 1996, p. 7). The will is the faculty of the mind that chooses good, loves God, desires God and is enabled to dwell in God. After the advent of human sin, the will can only do these things by God's grace (Wolters, 1978, p. 138). This intention, inspired by grace, overcomes the intellect's limitations and seeks the divine within the cloud of unknowing. Yet the intellect must continually be suppressed into the cloud of forgetting through tactics like a repeated word so that the higher spiritual level of the intention for union with the divine can be maintained over the lower spiritual good of the active intellect.

Prayer is viewed as most fundamentally about the setting of the will towards God to receive from God rather than an act of the intellect directing one's thoughts or petitions to God (Wolters, 1978, p. 106). Prayers for mature contemplatives are not planned but rather rise spontaneously and contain few if any words (Wolters, 197, p. 104). Prayer is primarily a sense of connection with or participation in the divine.

Humility is central to meditative contemplation; it is the process of seeing oneself truly. There are two sources of this correct vision of the self. One is a recognition of one's sinfulness and weakness. More important is the superabundance of God's love and goodness. The properly humble perspective occurs in only short durations, but in those moments it decentres the self in relation to the enormity of the divine. In recognising the self properly, it becomes possible to experience God (Wolters, 1978, p. 79). Having a proper sense of self clears the way for the surpassing experience of God.

In this humility of spirit, there is a movement towards nothingness. In contemplation, all but God is to be put to the side. The author urges, 'Try to suppress all knowledge and feeling of anything less than God, and trample it down deep under the cloud of forgetting' (Wolters, 1978, p. 110). Even awareness of one's own existence is to be crushed if contemplation is to reach its perfect state. This loss of awareness of self is the key moment in the contemplation, as it opens up an abyss of self in which all that is left is an empty nothingness. Into this abyss lies the opening to the cloud of unknowing of the ineffable God (Wolters, 1978, p. 144). This nothingness is not truly absence. Rather, 'to speak more accurately, it is overwhelming spiritual light that blinds the soul that is experiencing it, rather than actual darkness or the absence of physical light' (Wolters, 1978, p. 143). The nothingness is only nothingness to the intellect and outer senses, rather than to the spirit. Instead, within the nothing connection with God is found. The paradoxical experience of contemplation is that in nothingness the source of everything is itself experienced. The nothing is nothing but God, and yet when there is union with God, there is union with and love for everything (Meninger, 1996, p. 9).

The experience of nothingness is transformative. Not only is there a sense of one's sins washing away, but the infinity of God and divine love can be glimpsed to the extent humanly possible. In this, the symbolic nature of words about the divine grasped, as heaven is as much down as up or behind as before (Wolters, 1978, p. 134). In other words, the presence of God is imbued in the world as much as it is beyond the world. In this omnipresent divine all things are connected and all things are embraced in love. For the contemplative, the change that occurs is a participation in that love (Wolters, 1978, p. 93). This is the movement from intellect to will, experienced as a union with God and love for God and all others.

Prayer, in the meditative sense of the *Cloud,* is participation in love. Moreover, it is a sense of connection not only with God but with the entirety of the created world, which is discovered as being contained within God. Prayer is not primarily about words spoken, as that is an act of intellect, but rather about participation in the desire for union and the love that comes from the will.

Centring Prayer

The Cloud of Unknowing is the germinating text for the contemporary Christian spiritual practice of 'centring prayer.' The name is inspired by Merton's approach to meeting the divine by going into one's centre and passing from there to God (Pennington et al., 2012, p. 36.). The basic approach of the centring prayer model is to sit in silence to find God dwelling in the depths of one's inner being. Centring prayer follows the *Cloud* in having one's self undone to recognise a rootedness in God through techniques derived from the *Cloud* such as the use of repeated phrases to focus the mind, aiming to make the techniques accessible to non-monastics who are interested in Christian spiritual practices. At the same time, the sense of self that is decentred through centring prayer based on modern psychology, especially from a Freudian perspective.

Keating and Pennington both develop the details of centring prayer practice. Their writing is in the form of spiritual writing rather than academic writing, and so are more focused on clarity for a practitioner than depth of academic concepts. They do not follow the concepts of *The Cloud of Unknowing* in detail, but rather are inspired by the general approach in constructing centring prayer as a contemporary form of spiritual practice with roots in the mystical tradition of Christianity rather than direct application of the medieval practice. Keating (1999), for instance, develops the concept that the human condition is the experience of being without the presence of God. As God is always present but hidden in daily experience, the spiritual journey is the process of becoming aware of that divine presence. 'The problem', he notes, 'is that we only access that [divine] presence to the degree that our interior life is attuned to it' (p. 27). Spiritual practices are designed to deepen one's attunement to the divine presence.

Keating finds the concepts found in psychology to be of great importance for shaping spiritual disciplines. He points to the biological needs at birth – security and survival, power and control, affection and esteem – and notes that is not necessary to recognise the presence of God at that stage. Due to this, 'we build a universe with ourselves at the centre, around which all our human faculties revolve like planets around the sun' (Keating, 1999, p. 13). This viewpoint of the self at the centre serves as a basic diagnosis of the human condition for Keating, marking a contemporary definition of sin, or at least a key aspect of sin. This self as the centre is a false self that inevitably leads to misery because it is not centred in the presence of God.

In order to change the patterns of the false self, Keating (1999) contends that one needs to be willing to be exposed to one's unconscious. He holds, 'When we are not thinking, analysing, or planning and place ourselves in the presence of God in faith, we open ourselves to the contents of the unconscious' (p. 19). Keating continues that humility is needed in this opening of oneself to the unconscious, as the unconscious is a powerful realm of emotion that can overwhelm. It is the work of the Holy Spirit to transform our inmost being into a divine way of being through our engagement with the depths of the self. We can see in these contentions echoes of the *Cloud,* in that the intellect must be set aside in order to be open to the presence of God. At the same time, Keating places that experience in the category of the unconscious. In this way Keating draws on psychology while holding the spiritual journey as something that exceeds psychology.

Through an engagement and transformation of the self through contemplative silence that moves the self from the centre of existence, there is a spiritual experience of divine omnipresence, much like the author of the Cloud describes. Keating (1999) holds that because God is existence itself, God is present in everything that exists (p. 27). Divine presence, then, is the greatest reality and through being open to it everything in the universe becomes a reminder of God's presence. Through contemplation a transformation led by the Holy Spirit allows a recognition that God is always present and brings connection between all things that exist. This transformation is the growth of spiritual awareness. Yet Keating continues that the spiritual process is not primarily about a series of successful mystical experiences of ecstatic union with the divine. Rather, 'it is a series of humiliations of the false self that become more and more profound. These make room inside us for the Holy Spirit to come in and heal' (Keating, 1999, p. 38). It is specifically the failures of the false self that allow the unconscious to be faced and the divine presence to be recognised through the working of the Holy Spirit. A key work of the Holy Spirit in this understanding is emotional and psychological healing.

Pennington (2000), meanwhile, also describes the difference between a false self and a true self for centring prayer. Pennington also sets his description within a frame of psychology and infant identity formation. Pennington's focus, however, is on the ways that children experience love as conditional. For him the false self is a sense that the self is lovable only for what it does, accomplishes or possesses. Pennington (2000) construes the practice of centring prayer as effectively dying to this false self. The false self of doing is dislodged so that God is able to express divine being within us (p. 39). It is a humbling experience because the true self is recognised as the image and likeness of God. In this there is consonance with the sense in the *Cloud* that humility is especially found in recognising the abundance of the divine. More than just humility, the true self also recognises community, for 'we come to experience our true oneness with all in our common humanity and even more in our oneness in Christ the head of humanity. … We come to love our neighbours in truth as our very selves' (p. 47). In the emptiness of negating the (false) self, the abundance of God and neighbour is recognised. Pennington, like Keating, sees this experience as psychologically healing and leading to a desire to pursue what is good for the world as well as the self.

Centring prayer is widely practiced in the contemporary church. Its dependence on the themes of decentring the self into nothingness and then finding interconnection with others in finding union with God in that nothingness can be traced to the influence of the *Cloud*. At the same time, details such as discussion of the clouds of forgetting and unknowing are not emphasised. Rather, the focus is more on releasing false images of the self and opening what is hidden in the unconscious in order to free a space for connecting with the divine. While some attention is given to embodiment, such as suggestions for sitting comfortably and focusing on breath, centring prayer is still primarily an internal discipline and mental exercise. It does not, then, connect at least explicitly with social action or the connection of the self to technology, as postdigital prayer would need to do. Other frameworks are needed to add these dimensions.

The Cloud in Recent Academic Theology

Several recent constructive academic proposals have utilised concepts from *The Cloud of Unknowing*. The *Cloud* is sufficiently influential that a full catalogue of references to it is beyond the scope of this chapter. Rather, I wish to highlight several major works that draw on its themes in ways that support social engagement and ethical formation.

A significant contemporary engagement with the *Cloud of Unknowing* in contemporary theology comes from feminist liberation theologian Soelle in her late work on mystical theology, *The* Silent Cry (2001). In this work Soelle finds the metaphor of the 'cloud of forgetting' to be particularly valuable. While the *Cloud* writer is addressing a monastic situation and prioritising the contemplative life over the active one, Soelle directs the cloud of forgetting towards the realities of the poor. 'That cloud ... makes it possible for the poor to find joy in life, music, laughter' (p. 58). However, the cloud of forgetting is not simply a balm to allow life to be bearable to those in poverty. Rather, it liberates them from bondage to heteronomy and the powers that grip them such as hunger and infirmity. Thus she extends this spiritual practice of self-forgetting to defend against poverty being soul-crushing for those who do not endure it voluntarily. The cloud of forgetting becomes an essential step in resistance to oppressive forces such as economic ones. This is part of Soelle's larger project of overcoming the binary of contemplative and active in her construction of a socially activist theology grounded in mystical spirituality.

Feminist process theologian Keller (2015) builds on Soelle's reading of the cloud of forgetting as a call to practice a 'contemplative activism that also activates contemplation' (p. 83). Keller also points to Rudd's (2008) ecological reading of the *Cloud* as having an inclination towards interconnectedness resonant with contemporary ecological movements. Pickell (2018), meanwhile, argues for the *Cloud* as a model for contemporary Christian moral formation. Pickell notes that in the *Cloud,* the goal of prayer is understood to be cultivating a desire for God and aligning one's will towards God. He then traces this wordless approach to prayer as training for a kenotic releasing of control. In this kenotic posture, a dependence on the divine is recognised and cultivated, and such dependence lies at the root of moral formation.

In each of these recent works, contemplative prayer is understood to be intrinsically related to ethical action. While the works do not limit themselves to *The Cloud of Unknowing,* they draw on its themes as a key example of the contemplative tradition of Christian prayer. The cloud of forgetting then serves to speak of a stepping away from the structures of the world as it is so that a spiritual focus on the divine can be opened up. Within the following step of encountering the cloud of unknowing, meanwhile, allows for a sense of interconnection with God and the world while also empowering a divinely inspired love that can reach out into the world. Contemplation then becomes an empowering force for spiritually grounded social activism. Spirituality and engagement are shown to mutually enhance one another, highlighting the capacity of contemplative prayer to foster liberative action and reject the binary of theory and action, meeting the third and fourth criteria laid out in the introduction for postdigital prayer.

POSTDIGITAL SUBJECTIVITY

The first two criteria for postdigital prayer – overcoming the binary of digital/non-digital or human/technological and an understanding of subjectivity that extends beyond the physical and can include virtual aspects of the self – remain to be considered. Various theorists have been used as support for overcoming these separations. Donna Harraway's work on cyborg existence (Mansfield, 2000, pp. 158–161) is important for this topic, as is Maurice Merleau-Ponty's phenomenological concept of flesh that extends beyond the body (Liu, 2023). These additions are valuable. At the same time, I suggest that Guattari's formulation of machinic subjectivity is particularly suited to be employed in postdigital contemplative prayer. As centring prayer draws on the Freudian unconscious, Guattari's critique of that formulation of the unconscious and the independent self can open the practice of centring prayer and contemplative prayer in the *Cloud* tradition to a framework that is able to account for the technological as part of subjectivity.

Machinic Unconscious

Theorists Deleuze and Guattari worked to develop a theory of subjectivity that challenged the notion of coordinated selfhood. Rather, in their formulation a self is a collection of impulses and flows continually forming and re-forming in a momentary dynamic coalition experienced as a self (Mansfield, 2000, p. 136). They term this coalition an 'assemblage.' An assemblage is a collection of discrete objects that function together in a flow of interactivity that temporarily holds them together as having a type of unified existence while still also having multiple identities. A key aspect of their work is a challenge to the Freudian and Lacanian tradition of speaking of the unconscious, arguing instead for an alternative theory of the unconscious which they term *schizoanalysis* (Mansfield, 2000, p. 137).

Guattari's proposal in his individually authored works is to decentre the concept of the subject, focusing instead on a 'machinic subjectivity.' Rather than a conscious centre as the focus of a subject, for Guattari (1995) emphasising subjectivity means a focus on the relationship between subject and object and prioritising the intentionality between them (p. 22). This allows the self to be recognised as the nexus of objects and interactions that are momentarily contemporaneous. The identity of the subject, then, is found in its participation in the flow of events, objects and concepts that occur as an assemblage. The physical body or the mind of a human who experiences this assemblage as an 'I' joins in the participation of the subject but is not the extent of that subjectivity (Guattari, 1995, p. 25).

Subjectivity is related to participation in machines. Guattari has a particular understanding of 'machine' in this sense that is important to recognise. While machines are often considered to be a subset of technology, Guattari argues for reversing that order. He understands technology to be one form of machine. His concept of machine, however, extends beyond the technical, technological or material, even as some forms of machines do fit those categories. A machine, rather, is an ensemble that operates together. Machines that he terms 'material apparatus' are human-created machines that have material and energy components. These may include bulldozers, televisions, or smartphones. At the same time, he identifies abstract machines of various types. Physical bodies, social groups and institutional structures are machines in this sense (Guattari, 1995, p. 39). Abstract machines are assemblages in continual interaction (Guattari, 2011, p. 11).

Guattari's machines participate in subjectivity. An example he uses is watching television. The 'I' in this example sits at the intersection of several relationships. There is a relationship with the images on the screen. There is also a relationship with the narrative content coming from the show appearing on the screen. In addition to this relationship is an awareness of physical events occurring nearby, such as water boiling or other people in the room. There are also daydreams and ruminations. All of these function together in producing subjectivity; the technological device participates in this subjectivity as well as the human sense of being a self (Guattari, 1995, p. 16). Broader machines such as the language group that produces the television program and the arrangement of the room are also at work in this scenario. Since subjectivity comes from large-scale social machines as much as interior thoughts, Guattari is critical of the Freudian and Lacanian traditions of the unconscious. Rather, Guattari (2011) contends that the unconscious needs the addition of the machinic to effectively produce subjectivity (p. 10). Without the machinic sense of relationality the unconscious risks stagnation. In recasting the unconscious, Guattari advocates that the concept of unconscious only be considered for its production of subjectivity. Rather than seeing the unconscious as a realm of structure, language, emotion or other purely 'internal' constructions it should be understood as the realm of abstract machines that participate in the production of subjectivity in ways that move below the level of conscious awareness.

In considering electronic technologies, he suggests that AI and technological productions be seen as new sources for producing subjectivity in their capacity to interact (Guattari, 1995, p. 133). Technologies such as electronic devices have no meaning outside of the human intention that brings the technological devices into the subjectivity of that person, thus producing the meaning of the device. Building on Guattari, the virtual possibilities found online through the device then also participate in that subjectivity. In this way the subjectivity exceeds the materiality of the body and the materiality of the technological device. It includes not only the thoughts and concepts in that human mind, but also the possible concepts, relationships and interactions enabled through Internet participation. The virtual thus has an important role in the unconscious in its production of subjectivity. His conception that subjectivity must include the human relationship to digital technologies is one of the key values that his concepts of subjectivity and machines provide. To have postdigital subjectivity requires relationships mediated through technology that push beyond the boundaries of the physical into the realms of the virtual and the possible. As these technologies are integrated more and more seamlessly into everyday experience in the present and into the future, they will take on greater importance within the unconscious its production of subjectivity. The online experience of the self is an aspect of subjectivity, and the technology that enables this virtual dimension of subjectivity is an essential element of that subjectivity.

For Guattari, defining subjectivity has a political and ethical aspect. Hardt and Negri (2017, pp. 120–123) build on this insight, finding the concept of machinic subjectivity valuable because its sense of subjectivity held in common provides a model for political organising. It is a collective that is able to be diverse and dynamic, as it includes humans and non-humans in a common subjectivity. In rejecting the separation of the technological from humanity in human identity, a new sense of the common that incorporates material connections, knowledge, the technological and ecological into a common interconnected subjectivity emerges. This collective forms a basis for coalitions of resistance that form the foundation for their call to a new appreciation of the political and digital commons.

MACHINIC, THE POSTDIGITAL AND CONTEMPLATIVE PRAYER

The machinic unconscious is an effective understanding of subjectivity for a postdigital approach. It has an expansive sense of subjectivity that allows an expansion from an individual sense of self to a subjectivity that incorporates digital and online expressions of subjectivity, even recognising the role of technological devices as an integral part of that subjectivity. In this, the first two criteria I laid out as essential to my understanding of postdigital thought are met. Indeed, Hardt and Negri point to the political and social implications of the concept, thus meeting the third criterion. Machinic subjectivity, then, fully qualifies as a postdigital understanding of subjectivity. This is not to say that it is the only understanding of subjectivity that can be postdigital, but it is a view that is compatible with postdigital thought.

We can now return to the question of whether postdigital theory is compatible with Christian prayer. Can Guattari's machinic subjectivity be incorporated into a *Cloud*-influenced approach to contemplative prayer? There are some important similarities. In the *Cloud,* a central element of the prayer is the crushing of the self so that a connection with divine presence may emerge. In that union is a participation in divine love that can then be directed at all of creation, which is also found to be in God's presence. Machinic subjectivity also seeks to crush the self, at least as an individual self, in order to recognise relationality within an assemblage. This is an important resonance. To be sure it is not the same. For Guattari there is no connection to God, and so the crushing of the self is purely to recognise the relatedness within an assemblage. Such a relationship in an assemblage is a fleeting coalition and not an experience of being entangled with all of creation through unity in the divine.

Yet Keating adopted the concept of the unconscious to explain centring prayer without accepting all details of the discussion within psychology about the concept.

I suggest that the machinic unconscious can be a fount of constructive theological inspiration without needing to accept all of its details. For instance, the false self that Pennington described can be re-construed as being the sense of having an individual self. Such a separative self, as Keller (1988) terms it, is false because it does not recognise its deeply embedded relational nature. The flow of that relationality is found in the machinic unconscious.

Just as Keating ascribes the work of carefully opening the unconscious as a work of the Holy Spirit, I argue that opening to the machinic unconscious to recognise one's subjectivity as part of the flow of relationships in which it is entangled is a work of the Holy Spirit. Indeed, just as both Keating and Pennington see dislodging the self from the centre as an opportunity for emotional healing, I see the opening of the relational unconscious as a site of healing, particularly healing human connections with one another, with the earth and with destructive relationships with technology. Such forms of healing may be the more pressing need for healing at this time than the emotional healing that was at the forefront of the context addressed by Keating and Pennington.

As the Holy Spirit opens us to our subjectivity within the machinic unconscious it enables seeing the presence of the divine, symbolically allowing a sense of ascending to God in recognising the God who is already everywhere and involved in the mutual connections and relationality of our subjectivity assemblages. This, in turn, opens a sense of relationship with all through God, not just our immediate assemblage. This is a participation in love that includes all: physical, virtual, online, technological, AI, animal, fungus and more. All are the realm in which God is seen to operate because all are part of the divine subjectivity.

Postdigital Cloud Prayer

Returning to the opening question, what contribution might prayer make to postdigital Christian theology and spirituality? This is in part a practical question of what postdigital prayer might look like or how to go about it. I suggest first that it is *Cloud*-based prayer, drawing on the themes and concerns of *The Cloud of Unknowing*. The practice of this prayer would look externally quite similar to current centring prayer practices. Tactics such as sitting comfortably, focusing on breathing and having a centring phrase all remain. It is the understanding of the initial conditions that has the most substantial difference.

The primary differences between centring prayer and postdigital prayer come prior to the cloud of forgetting. The cloud of forgetting is not prominent in discussions of centring prayer, but ruminations on the false self, the human condition and the unconscious serve within centring prayer for explanations of what is to be released in the cloud of forgetting. It is a tailoring of the concept to the needs of the audience being addressed by centring prayer, adapting the *Cloud* author's goal in this cloud of releasing material concerns. In postdigital cloud prayer, what is to be released is the fallacy of the separative self, the division of digital and physical and the separation between human and non-human. Keeping Soelle in mind are the structures that lessen the value of some subjectivities over others. Liberation from artificial hierarchies of wealth, gender expression, race, sexual orientation and attitudes of ecological exploitation, to name but a few, is found in the cloud of forgetting.

As these realities of a postdigital condition are released, the notion of a self is decentred so that a space in which God might be encountered is opened. This crushing of the self and opening to God is the work of the Holy Spirit given by grace. In it, the machinic unconscious is opened so that a recognition of participation in the flow of subjectivity can be glimpsed, if only briefly. In this glimpse is a participation in love that provides a space for aligning the will with God in moral formation.

CONCLUSION

The alignment of the will with God and moral formation includes a recognition of digital spaces as imbued with the indwelling of God. This means that virtual realities, online worlds and universes, AI, embodied technologies and social media are all held within the divine presence and are spaces in which God is present. Due to this, such prayer means that part of the preparation that occurs in the contemplative silence is to focus awareness on the digital aspects of the online cloud of one's subjectivity so that the Holy Spirit may move through those aspects as well, dynamically opening them up to connection and newness as part of the movement through the cloud of forgetting into the cloud of unknowing. In that cloud the divine ineffability that contains and surpasses all of the other clouds – physical, digital, of forgetting – can be experienced, even if only briefly and imperfectly. In this we see the contribution of prayer to postdigital theology.

REFERENCES

Clarke, K. (2019). Words and silence: On reading revelations of divine love and the cloud of unknowing. *The Way*, 58(2), 93–109.

Fawns, T., Ross, J., Carbonel, H., Noteboom, J., Finnegan-Dehn, S., & Raver, M. (2023). Mapping and tracing the postdigital: Approaches and parameters of postdigital research. *Postdigital Science and Education*, 5, 623–642. https://doi.org/10.1007/s42438-023-00391-y

Guattari, F. (1995). *Chaosmosis: An ethico-aesthetic paradigm* (P. Bains & J. Pefanis, Trans.). Sydney: Power.

Guattari, F. (2011). *The machinic unconscious: Essays in schizoanalysis*. Los Angeles, CA: Semiotext(e).

Hardt, M., & Negri, A. (2017). *Assembly*. New York: Oxford University Press.

Keating, K. (1999). *The human condition: Contemplation and transformation*. New York: Paulist Press.

Keller, C. (1988). *From a broken web: Separation, sexism, and self.* Boston, MA: Beacon Press.

Keller, C. (2015). *Cloud of the impossible: Negative theology and planetary entanglement*. New York: Columbia University Press.

Liu, Z. (2023). Internet of bodies, datafied embodiment and our quantified religious future. *HTS Teologiese Studies/Theological Studies*, 79, 1–12. https://doi.org/10.4102/hts.v79i1.8398.

Mansfield, N. (2000). *Subjectivity: Theories of the self from Freud to Haraway*. New York University Press.

McLaren, P., & Jandrić, P. (2020). *Postdigital dialogues on critical pedagogy, liberation theology and information technology*. London: Bloomsbury.

Meninger, W. A. (1996). *The loving search for God: Contemplative prayer and The Cloud of Unknowing*. New York: Continuum.

Pennington, M. B., Keating, T., & Clarke, T. E. (2012). *Finding grace at the center: The beginning of centering* prayer (3rd ed.). Nashville: Turner Publishing Company.

Pennington, M. D. (2000). *True self, false self: Unmasking the spirit within*. New York: Crossroad.

Pickell, T. R. (2018). Gentle space-making: Christian silent prayer, mindfulness, and kenotic identity formation. *Studies in Christian Ethics*, 32(1), 66–77. https://doi.org/10.1177/0953946818808142

Radde-Antweiler, K. (2022). Embodiment. In H. A. Campbell & R. Tsuria (Eds.), *Digital religion: Understanding religious practice in digital media* (2nd ed.). pp. 103–119. London: Routledge.

Rudd, G. (2008). From popular science to contemplation: The clouds of The Cloud of Unknowing. In S. Ruston (Ed.), *Literature and science*. pp. 13–33. Woodbridge, Suffolk, UK: English Association.

Soelle, D. (2001). *The silent cry: Mysticism and resistance*. (B. Rumscheidt & M. Rumscheidt, Trans). Minneapolis: Fortress Press.

Wolters, C. (1978). *The Cloud of Unknowing, and other works*. New York: Penguin Classics.

5 The Postdigital Church
Implications of the Concept of Postdigitality for Current Research on the Digital Church

Sabrina Müller and Aline Knapp

INTRODUCTION

This chapter argues that the 'postdigital church' should not be understood as a present description of the institution of the church, but rather as a specific research perspective that focuses on Internet users and their understanding of the church within their postdigital lifeworld. It begins by exploring the idea of postdigital life and examines the shift in the perception of online and offline in research on digital churches. This chapter also discusses how this research strand relates to previous research conducted on the topic of the digital church. This is exemplified through the phenomena of religious apps and pastoral influencers and asks to what extent it is appropriate to speak of a postdigital church and what exactly this term means.

OVERVIEW: POSTDIGITAL LIFE

In recent years, I (Sabrina) have frequently worked with regional churches and congregations in both Germany and Switzerland, training clergy and church leaders, and often addressing questions regarding digitalisation and the church. Within this context, online and offline are still seen as separate worlds, with the digital realm being primarily related to media. This conception can also (at least implicitly) be seen in certain research strands (see Section on 'Media Use of Churches'). However, this understanding is increasingly being complemented by an alternative conception of the digital that emphasises the fluidity between offline and online, focuses much more on the user perspective and can be described as postdigital.

The understanding that online and offline are still seen as separate worlds overlooks the fact that modern human existence is more intertwined with technology than ever before, with technology influencing every aspect of daily life. This is particularly evident with the smartphone, a device that accompanies modern Western individuals in nearly all life situations (sometimes 24 hours a day). 'Mobile phones

DOI: 10.1201/9781003497950-7

are an indispensable part of modern life, as they have evolved from communication tools to multifunctional devices, which can satisfy all kinds of needs ranging from learning to entertaining' (Lou, Deng & Wang, 2022, p. 3191). The ubiquity of the smartphone extends to the point where the device has increasingly become an extension of the self.

> [The] relationship between smartphones and humans can be viewed from an extended-self perspective – smartphones extend the human self beyond the human body, and smartphones are becoming part of the 'human self'.
>
> *(Singh & Munderia, 2022, p. 113)*

This ongoing development of the smartphone as an integral component and extension of the self underscores the deep intertwining of human beings and technology. The increased integration of digital tools with the self significantly affects self-conception, interpersonal dynamics and the perception of individual identity (Vgl. Lou, Han, Wang & Pei, 2022, pp. 15–17).

The ubiquity of the smartphone blurs the boundaries between online and offline. This merging of spheres is increasingly discussed using the term 'postdigital', which is multifaceted and has undergone a shift in meaning since 2015. While the term partly aims to describe the relationship between online and offline, it now primarily expresses the notion that the virtual world is increasingly merging with daily life, making these two realms scarcely distinguishable.

> We now live in a postdigital world where digital technology and media is [no longer] separate, virtual, 'other' to a 'natural' human and social life. [...] The postdigital approach does not seek technical innovation or improvement, but considers digitisation as something that has already happened and, thus, might be further reconfigured [...]. The postdigital is hard to define: messy, unpredictable, digital and analogue, technological and non-technological; biological and informational. The postdigital is both a rupture in our existing theories and their continuation [...].
>
> *(Jandrić & Hayes, 2020, p. 288)*

In research on digital religion and theology, Maggi Savin-Baden and John Reader have also pointed out that humans and technologies are increasingly shaping each other, making it increasingly difficult to draw clear lines between these two worlds. In line with Savin-Baden and Reader, the term 'postdigital' thus refers to the continuous and nearly indistinguishable blending of once clearly separable online and offline realms (Savin-Baden & Reader, 2022, p. xii).

STATE OF RESEARCH: DIGITAL CHURCH

As an evolution of the term 'digital church', the concept of the 'postdigital church' cannot be understood independently from the existing field of research on the digital church. Therefore, the following section will first provide a brief overview of the current state of research. This is less about evaluating previous research and more about providing an overview that aims to clarify what the concept 'postdigital' contributes to existing research.

The interdisciplinary discourse on the digital church can be categorised into three different research strands: (1) Research into online religious communities, (2) media use of churches and (3) digital ecclesiology.

These three strands will be presented in more detail in the following subsections through exemplary works. All three follow a somewhat chronological development, with the study of religious communities being one of the earliest topics in the field of digital religions, while the concept of digital ecclesiology and, thus, theological reflections on the nature and essence of the church are significantly more recent (Campbell & Dyer, 2021, p. 9). This aligns with Phillips et al.'s observation that digital theology, like digital religion, is 'still in its infancy in comparison with digital humanities' (Phillips, Schiefelbein-Guerrero & Kurlberg, 2019, p. 36). However, it is by no means apparent that these research strands are replacing each other. Instead, they continue to co-exist and form a multifaceted research discourse on the digital church.

Research on Religious Communities Online

The research strand on digital religious communities is one of the oldest topics in the interdisciplinary field of digital religion. In conjunction with the discourse on virtual communities, research on religious communities started to emerge as early as the late 1990s (Campbell & Sheldon, 2022, p. 72). Since then, this research strand has undergone various stages and addressed different research questions, which Heidi Campbell compares to the waves of research conducted on the concept of digital religion as a whole (Campbell & Sheldon, 2022, pp. 76–81; Campbell & Vitullo, 2016, p. 74).

Early studies focused on the question of whether online groups could be considered *communities* at all, and in a second step, whether they could be considered *religious* communities. Various studies quickly demonstrated

> that religious communities online could be viewed by members as authentic, though representing a new form often quite different in their social and communicative practices than traditional religious communities.
>
> *(Campbell & Vitullo, 2016, pp. 83–84)*

Consequently, a second research question became increasingly relevant: how to define and characterise the diverse online communities. 'This created a new wave of research that identified and compared different typologies or forms of online community' (Campbell & Sheldon, 2022, p. 78). Campbell, for instance, characterised six 'traits that draw people to a specific online group and encourage their investment in it' (Campbell, 2020, p. 50). These six traits were: A network of relationships, giving and receiving care and support, self-esteem, connections that feel authentic as well as safe and shared beliefs (Campbell, 2020, p. 50).

Due to the focus on online communities, this discourse has long assumed a separation between online and offline contexts. However, it is becoming increasingly clear, in this research strand, that a strong dichotomy between online and offline communities cannot be maintained. 'In stage three, scholars began to highlight the ways in which online and offline communities could and should be seen as part of a continuum' (Campbell & Vitullo, 2016, p. 84).

Media Use of Churches

A second major research strand addresses the question of how, and to what extent, existing church institutions make use of digital media. Although this strand has been around for some time (for instance, the following article about the usage of digital tools in youth community Ojala, 2017), it has experienced a massive surge due to the global pandemic.

Due to COVID-19, there has been a massive increase in the use of digital formats and offerings within churches across Europe. The digitisation of the church manifested in the continuation of regular worship services in a digital format. During the lockdown, a significant amount of energy was dedicated to maintaining Sunday worship services digitally in the institutionalised church practices in both Germany and Switzerland. In a short period of time, almost every local congregation established an online worship service that was often live-streamed from empty churches. Thus, clergy staged the Sunday worship service in the church for viewers who were tuning in via their screens. This practice has persisted, particularly in larger congregations, up to 2024. Worship services and devotions were most commonly celebrated. Telephone devotions were also significant and mostly used by elderly people, while participative formats were rarely practiced (Müller, 2022b; Oorschot, 2020).

Several predominantly quantitative studies have addressed the question of how the institutionalised church acted digitally during the pandemic. Notable among these are the CONTOC study (Churches Online in Times of Corona), (Schlag et al., 2023a), a study about Digital Education (Müller & Bruderer-Traber, 2023), the Midi study (Hörsch, 2022) and the ReTeOG study (Sievert & Reimann, 2021). However, the largest international study in this context is the CONTOC study, which examined the digitalisation processes utilised in churches throughout Switzerland, Germany and Austria and provides insights into seven other countries through so-called country reports (Schlag et al., 2023b). The CONTOC study provides a multitude of mainly quantitative results on the digital church. Pastors were asked to what extent they used digital media in their various fields of action, such as worship, pastoral care, education and social welfare during the pandemic. As a result, this study offers a comprehensive picture of the digital offerings of various churches during this time.

While the research discourse on religious communities primarily focuses on the perspective of religious groups that formed online, this research strand began with existing institutionalised churches and examined their use of digital media, as exemplified by the CONTOC study. In this research strand, the term 'digitality' is used less as a comprehensive cultural concept, as suggested by terms like 'postdigital', 'digital age' or 'digital condition' (Stalder, 2018), but is rather narrowed down to refer to digital media. While it is crucial to acknowledge that the CONTOC study takes into account this cultural understanding of digitality, it nevertheless focuses on digitality in terms of digital media (Schlag et al., 2023b, pp. 6–7).

Digital Ecclesiology

The third research strand deals with the theological question of the essence or nature of the church and the transformation of certain theologoumena within the processes of digitalisation in the church. Campbell and Dyer argue

> Digital ecclesiology is focused on more than simply discussing [...] doing church online [...] it is not a 'how to' for church online, nor is it about debates, such as the authenticity of virtual [...] community in online religious platforms. [...] The purpose [...] is to address the broader and deeper issues and questions that are emerging from churches' digital experimentation.
>
> *(Campbell & Dyer, 2021, pp. 10–11)*

Research in this field is generally less empirical and more interpretative or hermeneutical in nature. One of the most frequently discussed and polarising topics within this strand, in recent years, has been Holy Communion. This topic has also been significantly influenced by the COVID-19 pandemic and the political regulations imposed to ensure social distancing. Since the appropriate celebration of the Holy Communion is considered a central defining characteristic of the church, according to CA 7 (Confessio Augustana), the debate entails a deeply ecclesiological concern (Todjeras, 2020, pp. 65–66). Current theological discussions revolve around the question of whether the Eucharist can be appropriately conveyed via digital means (Todjeras, 2020, p. 56). One of the central problems discussed in various denominations has been the question of whether virtual gatherings qualify as embodied communities, for example, Bentley suggests:

> Church polity on Holy Communion assumes that the status quo for Holy Communion is a physical gathering, where the celebrant, elements, and congregation are present as an act of community.
>
> *(Bentley, 2021, p. 4)*

What this example highlights is that the church is frequently conceptualised as an offline institution in this research strand. Such a stance underscores the issues that offline and online spaces continue to be regarded as distinct entities, rather than part of an interwoven continuum.

EXPLORING THE POSTDIGITAL CHURCH

The central thesis of this chapter is that the concept of postdigitality currently manifests primarily in the individual, who, for example, through the constant use of smartphones, has synchronised the online and offline worlds to such an extent that finding a clear distinction between these realms is no longer possible as mentioned earlier.

As the aforementioned examples illustrate, there is still a noticeable distinction between online and offline formats within church institutions worldwide, and sometimes even a devaluation of digital formats compared to offline settings (Todjeras, 2020, pp. 63–64). Postdigital, therefore, does not denote a characteristic of the church as an institution.

This also means that the research questions of the three presented research strands remain relevant and cannot yet be considered answered. In other words, they require ongoing research.

The term ‘postdigital church’ is used here to denote a fourth research strand that focuses less on the institutional logic of the church and more on the perspective of the participants. It aims to examine church from the perspective of recipients and users. This demand is not inherently new but often receives insufficient attention in current debates on the digital church, as demonstrated above.

Taking on this perspective has two consequences. First, it leads to different research questions, as will be demonstrated during the discussion about religious influencers. Second, it brings other phenomena into focus that are not necessarily apparent from an institutional logic, as will be demonstrated using the example of religious apps.

The Postdigital Church as a Way of Asking Research Questions: The Example of Religious Influencers

In the German-speaking context, there is a growing phenomenon of church-related religious influencers who are highly engaged and active on Instagram (Müller, 2022a; Müller & Knapp, 2022; Müller, 2024). Behind this phenomenon are church representatives with remarkable reach on social media. It is mostly clergy or vicars who the initiative to become active on social media platforms, allowing them to network and, thus, gain visibility within a networked public. In the context of digital logic (Klinger & Svensson, 2015; van Dijck & Poell, 2013), several profound shifts are evident. Notably, there has been a transformation in global perceptions (Rosa, 2016, p. 716) and a decline in the significance of traditional institutions (Serres, 2013, p. 23). Additionally, increased access to information and the hybridisation of life (Consalvo & Ess, 2012) contribute to the erosion of boundaries between the private and public spheres. This blending of spheres is a critical aspect of our contemporary digital landscape (Schmidt & Cohen, 2013, p. 56). The integration of digital technologies into everyday life facilitates constant connectivity and interaction, thereby reshaping how individuals engage with both personal and societal structures.

Drawing on Campbell’s distinction of ‘religious digital creatives’, which further divides these individuals into ‘digital entrepreneurs’, ‘spokespersons’, and ‘strategists’, the influencers described here can be categorised as strategists. Entrepreneurs are individuals with a technical background who typically volunteer in a church. Meanwhile, spokespersons refer specifically to employed social media experts that work for a given organisation. ‘Digital strategists’ are individuals with a religious ‘calling’ or ordination, such as a nun, monk or clergy member (Campbell, 2021).

Church influencers provide insight into highly personal everyday experiences, while simultaneously acting in their official capacity as clergy, for example, by posting pictures in clerical attire or with a clerical collar. They pray and conduct devotions on Instagram or YouTube, as well as post short liturgical elements and private moments. Through the posts, the social media community can participate in their pastoral and family life, as well as their doubts, failures and successes.

The same phenomenon can now be studied from two perspectives. From an institutional logic, which, as shown, prevails in the discourse on the digital church, the phenomenon can be compared with offline settings: Which pastoral activities are the pastoral influencers carrying out on Instagram? Is pastoral care, for instance, taking place here? To what extent can the Instagram posts be understood as sermons?

While these questions are undoubtedly still of great relevance, they can be complemented by a different line of inquiry when, from the perspective of a postdigital logic, questions are asked more from the followers' point of view rather than the institution's perspective:

- The followers are placed at the centre as autonomous actors who decide on their form of religiosity and religious communication. Users choose whom to follow, where and how to interact, like, comment or whom to unfollow.
- Possible research questions in this perspective could be: to what extent does the followers' spirituality benefit from the influencers' output? What and how are (religious) experiences shaped by the various posts and reels of the influencers? To what extent, and in what ways, do followers experience church in these contexts?
- It becomes evident that, from this perspective, there is less emphasis on comparing online and offline settings, and instead, the social media context is regarded more earnestly as an integral part of the followers' lived experience and everyday life.

The Postdigital Church as an Examination of Non-Institutional Practices: The Example of Religious Apps

There are countless fascinating examples in this segment, but we will focus on religious and spiritual apps. The usage of religious apps '[…] constitutes part of an increasingly diverse range of religious practices that often fall outside traditional thinking' (Scott, 2016, p. 255). Apps are particularly interesting in relation to the proposed research field, as the dichotomy between online and offline worlds is 'bridged by the ubiquity of mobile apps that – through portability, ease of access, continuous presence, technological networks and a broad scope of interaction – foster experiences unique among digital technologies' (Fewkes, 2019, p. 6).

Together with Patrick Todjeras, we have been immersed in the field of app research for four years. During this time, we have examined apps from regional churches in addition to well-being apps available on the open market.

The use of spiritual and religious apps has experienced a significant increase in recent years. For example, Google announced that, between 2019 and 2020, search queries for yoga and meditation apps increased by 65% (Top meditation app statistics you need to know in 2024, Kaur, 2024). Even during the pandemic, the download rate of these apps increased massively. Sensor Tower, a company specialising in app store intelligence, found that, in April 2020, 2 million more mindfulness apps were downloaded than in January of that same year. The leading apps were 'Calm' (with 3.9 million downloads), 'Headspace' (with 1.5 million downloads) and 'Meditopia' (with 1.4 million downloads) in April 2020. Additionally, apps like 'Reflectly', 'Daylio', 'Relax' and 'Insight Timer' also gained significant popularity. During April 2020, the total number of downloads of wellness apps was estimated at 10 million, representing a 24.2% increase ('Downloads of Top English-Language Mental Wellness Apps Surged by 2 Million in April Amid COVID-19 Pandemic', n.d.). Since 2015, more than 2,500 meditation apps have been developed, (Kaur, (2024). Top meditation app statistics you need to know in 2024) rooted either in a specific denomination or religion, or being inter- or trans-religious (Kaur, (2024). Top meditation app statistics you need to know in 2024). People download these apps in the hope of achieving spiritual well-being, receiving religious inspiration and obtaining support for their mental health.

Since 2021 I (Sabrina) have been examining the dynamics of Insight Timer as a participant observer and participating in various circles or groups. Insight Timer (Inc, n.d.) is one of the leading meditation apps, which provides a wide range of meditative resources and tools to promote personal well-being. This combination of different features makes Insight Timer a comprehensive offering for spiritual seekers, as well as for beginners and experienced practitioners in the field of meditation. Religion through an app is planned and controllable. Depending on one's availability, one can engage in a five or 15-minute meditation alone or as part of a group. Depending on one's inclination, this meditation can be practiced in the form of a Hindu mantra, a breathing meditation by Thích Nhất Hạnh or as a Christian contemplative prayer. Through the smartphone, access to religion-related practices and religious proclamations is held in one's own hands. Religious practices are initiated through religious apps, which can shape and potentially alter one's personal frame of reference throughout one's everyday life (Bellar, 2017, p. 114). This is reflected, for example, in the following feedback on the religious app Evermore: 'Thank you very much for this valuable app. It helps me become more aware of God's presence in my everyday life and it helps me take the step into the digital world, which I had previously rejected as meaningless' (Evermore Feedback Emails 2020–2021: 10|195-10|195). Evermore is a religious app developed by the Evangelical Lutheran Church of Hanover. It is further researched by Aline as part of her doctoral thesis. Following the concept of 'postdigital church' Aline is particularly interested in user experiences with the app and the characteristics of the spirituality that emerges. Using a Grounded Theory approach, she examines these user experiences through the methodology of experience sampling. During the data-collection process, users of Evermore compared the app with faith courses, religious inspirations and church services. In certain cases, Evermore does replace Christian community and become a place of worship (Merian et al., 2024).

This specialisation is also evident in the multireligious app, Insight Timer (IT), which not only facilitates individual spiritual practice, but also communal meditations, chats and the ability to follow so-called spiritual teachers. This connection of community and belonging in apps has been scarcely researched to date, but is central to their use, as illustrated by the following statement from a 50-year-old woman on Insight Timer:

> We've been on IT since 2014 or 2015, I think. We used it for meditations, which were really helpful. I have to say, though, that since we joined the XY Circle in March, my

> time meditating has skyrocketed. I think it is in part because of the dynamics of group meditation and the heart connection we have with people all over the globe [...] I guess what I am saying is the personal connection has taken our use of this app to a whole other level.

Moreover, Insight Timer exemplifies how religious content can dissolve into a trans-religious experience, blending various spiritual traditions and practices into a cohesive digital environment. The app offers an extensive range of meditations and teachings that transcend specific religious boundaries, appealing to users who are seeking a more universal spiritual experience. This fluidity between the 'online' and 'offline' realms blurs the traditional boundaries of religious practice. Users often describe a seamless integration of their digital spiritual activities with their everyday lives, suggesting that these apps are not merely tools for isolated meditation, but are becoming integral components of their spiritual journeys.

Religious apps clearly illustrate how religious practices are becoming more individualised, fluid and diversified. Religious communication is not only becoming more commonplace and participatory, but also more permeable to the traditional boundaries between religions and the secular and sacred (Tsuria, 2021, pp. 1–3; Knoblauch, 2009, pp. 38–80, 265–284.)

OUTLOOK: THE POSTDIGITAL CHURCH AS A FURTHER RESEARCH STRAND

The smartphone, a typical artefact of the postdigital world, is gaining spiritual significance (Muralidharan, Ferle & Roth-Cohen, 2023). Within the research strand of the postdigital church, as suggested in this article, users come to the fore as actors who hold religious authority by choosing religious apps, following and unfollowing, commenting, liking and posting on social media, etc. Through the diverse religious offerings available on smartphones, technology is increasingly integrated into daily spiritual life. Everyday places (traditionally not considered spiritual sites) become venues for spiritual experiences through digital platforms. For example, the home environment becomes a space for meditation and spiritual community. This causes the boundaries between the material and the immaterial worlds to blur. New forms of everyday spirituality, which seemed unthinkable just a few decades ago, thrive in this context. Thus, new opportunities for individual and communal spiritual experiences have emerged, where boundaries between online and offline, as well as secular and sacred, spaces are dissolved. This fusion blurs traditional clarities and demarcations in spiritual practice, creating a dynamic interaction between the various spheres of life. It is a new form of shared religious-spiritual practices that is observed here.

By focusing on the users' perspective and viewing the church less from the institution's perspective and more from that of the participants, this line of research shows remarkable similarities to the field of lived theology (Müller, 2021; Tveitereid, 2023; Marsh, Slade & Azaransky, 2016). If users are increasingly researched and viewed as theological actors within a postdigital church, this line of inquiry contributes to the central concerns of lived theology.

> The subject orientation in practical theology [...] expands in such an approach that the subject not only comes into view, but becomes a constructive and productive agent of theology.
>
> *(Müller, 2023, p. 218)*

The research strand on the postdigital church has the opportunity not only to conduct descriptive research, but also to contribute to the empowerment of various individuals in a culture of digitality by increasingly focusing on their perspectives.

CONCLUSION

In this chapter, the concept 'postdigital church' has been proposed as a research strand complementing the ongoing discourse on digital church.

Currently, the term 'postdigital church' cannot be understood as an adequate description of the institution of the church, as there is often a strong distinction made between online and offline practices in church practice, with offline practices frequently being devalued as inferior. Previous research on digital church has primarily focused on various facets of the institutionalised church: How does it use media? What theological implications does this media usage have for the nature of the church, and to what extent can online offerings be considered a church community?

The concept 'postdigital church' aims to expand and complement this research by focusing on the users and participants of digital religious practices. Postdigitality, as the central argument of the article suggests, primarily describes individual realities where online and offline spheres blur, especially through the use of smartphones. The research strand on postdigital church examines church from the perspective of the postdigital life world of the users, bringing new research questions and new phenomena into focus.

REFERENCES

Bellar, W. (2017). Private Practice: Using Digital Diaries and Interviews to Understand Evangelical Christians' Choice and Use of Religious Mobile Applications. *New Media & Society*, 19 (1), 111–125.

Bentley, W. (2021). Celebrating the Sacrament of Holy Communion During COVID-19: A Methodist Perspective. *HTS Teologiese Studies/Theological Studies*, 77 (4), 1–8.

Campbell, H. A. (2020). What Religious Groups Need to Consider When Trying to Do Church Online. In H. A. Campbell (Ed.), *The Distanced Church: Reflections on Doing Church Online* (pp. 49–52). Digital Religion Publications. https://oaktrust.library.tamu.edu/server/api/core/bitstreams/fcc63701-dc5d-4d8e-8ae8-2bb29cd4c513/content

Campbell, H. A., & Dyer, J. (2021). Introduction: What Does a Conversation on Digital Ecclesiology Look like? In H. A. Campbell & J. Dyer (Eds.), *Ecclesiology for a Digital Church. Theological Reflections on a New Normal* (pp. 8–14). London: SCM Press.

Campbell, H. A., & Sheldon, Z. (2022). Community. In H. A. Campbell & R. Tsuria (Eds.), *Digital Religion. Understanding Religious Practice in Digital Media* (2nd ed., pp. 71–86). London: Routledge.

Campbell, H. A., & Vitullo, A. (2016). Assessing Changes in the Study of Religious Communities in Digital Religion Studies. *Church, Communication and Culture*, 1 (1), 73–89.

Consalvo, M., & Ess, C. (2012). Introduction. In M. Consalvo & C. Ess (Eds.), *The Handbook of Internet Studies* (pp. 1–8). Malden, MA: Wiley-Blackwell.

Craig, C., (2020). Downloads of Top English-Language Mental Wellness Apps Surged by 2 Million in April Amid COVID-19 Pandemic. Retrieved 22 January 2022, from https://sensortower.com/blog/top-mental-wellness-apps-april-2020-downloads.

Fewkes, J. H. (2019). Piety in the Pocket: An Introduction. In J. H. Fewkes (Ed.), *Anthropological Perspectives on the Religious Uses of Mobile Apps* (pp. 1–16). Cham: Springer International Publishing.

Hörsch, D. (Ed.) (2022). *Midi-Studie: Digitale verkündigungs-formate während der corona-Krise. Eine Ad-hoc-Studie im Auftrag der Evangelischen Kirche in Deutschland* (2nd ed.). Berlin: midi.

Jandrić, P., & Hayes, S. (2020). Postdigital We-Learn. *Studies in Philosophy and Education*, 39, 285–297.

Kaur, G., (2024). Top meditation app statistics you need to know in 2024. Retrieved 28 Mai 2025, from: https://bigohtech.com/top-meditation-app-statistics.

Klinger, U., & Svensson, J. (2015). The Emergence of Network Media Logic in Political Communication: A Theoretical Approach. *New Media & Society*, 17 (8), 1241–1257.

Knoblauch, H. (2009). *Populäre Religion: Auf dem Weg in eine spirituelle Gesellschaft.* Frankfurt am Main: Campus Verlag.

Lou, J., Deng, L., & Wang, D. (2022). Understanding the Deep Structure Use of Mobile Phones – an Attachment Perspective. *Behaviour & Information Technology*, 41 (15), 3191–3209.

Lou, J., Han, N., Wang, M. D., & Pei, X. (2022). Effects of Mobile Identity on Smartphone Symbolic Use: An Attachment Theory Perspective. *International Journal of Environmental Research and Public Health, 19* (21), 1–20.

Marsh, C., Slade, P., & Azaransky, S. (2016). *Lived Theology: New Perspectives on Method, Style, and Pedagogy* (Illustrated Edition). New York: Oxford University Press.

Merian, K., Knapp, A., Todjeras, P., & Müller, S. (2024). Apps als spirituelle Impulsgeberinnen? Einsichten aus einem partizipativen Citizen Science-Projekt zur App EVERMORE. *Praktische Theologie*, 24 (2), 111–120.

Müller, S. (2021). *Lived Theology: Impulses for a Pastoral Theology of Empowerment.* Eugene, OR: Cascade Books.

Müller, S. (2022a). Öffentliche Kommunikation christlicher Sinnfluencer:innen. *Pastoraltheologie*, 111 (6), 203–218.

Müller, S. (2022b). Predigen im Kontext digitaler Dynamiken. *Epd Dokumentation*, 37, 12–21.

Müller, S. (2023). *Religious Experience and its Transformational Power: Qualitative and Hermeneutic Approaches to a Practical Theological Foundational Concept.* Boston, MA: De Gruyter.

Müller, S. (2024). Glaubensinfluencer:innen auf Instagram. In V. Pirker & P. Paschke (Eds.), *Religion auf Instagram: Analysen und Perspektiven* (pp. 137–153). Freiburg i. Breisgau: Verlag Herder.

Müller, S., & Bruderer-Traber, N. (2023). Smart Theology and Social Competency: Navigating Youth Engagement in the Digital Age. *Ecclesial Practices*, 10 (1), 5–17.

Müller, S., & Knapp, A. (2022). Praktisch Theologische Einordnung der Studie. In D. Hörsch (Ed.), *Digitale Communities. Eine Pilotstudie zur Followerschaft von christlichen Influencer*innen auf Instagram* (pp. 61–70). Berlin: midi.

Muralidharan, S., Ferle, C. L., & Roth-Cohen, O. (2023). The Digitalization of Religion: Smartphone Use and Subjective Well-Being during COVID-19. *Journal for the Scientific Study of Religion,* 62 (1), 144–163.

Ojala, E. (2017). What Happens in a Youth Community of Learning When Mobile Technology Is Implemented? The Case of a Finnish Evangelical-Lutheran Church Confirmation Training. *International Journal of Practical Theology*, 21 (2), 215–239.

Oorschot, F. van. (2020). Präsent sein. Ekklesiologische Perspektiven auf das kirchliche Leben unter den Bedingungen des Infektionsschutzes und seiner Folgen. *Cursor_Zeitschrift Für Explorative Theologie*. Retrieved 28 May 2024, from https://cursor.pubpub.org/pub/2k2hdjci/release/1.

Phillips, P., Schiefelbein-Guerrero, K., & Kurlberg, J. (2019). Defining Digital Theology: Digital Humanities, Digital Religion and the Particular Work of the CODEC Research Centre and Network. *Open Theology*, 5 (1), 29–43.

Rosa, H. (2016). *Resonanz: Eine Soziologie der Weltbeziehung* (5th ed.). Berlin: Suhrkamp Verlag.

Savin-Baden, M., & Reader, J. (Eds.). (2022). *Postdigital Theologies: Technology, Belief, and Practice*. Cham: Springer International Publishing AG.

Schlag, T., Nord, I., Beck, W., Bünker, A., Lämmlin, G., Müller, S., Pock, J., & Rothgangel, M. (2023a). *Churches Online in Times of Corona: Die CONTOC-Studie: Empirische Einsichten, Interpretationen und Perspektiven*. Wiesbaden: Springer VS.

Schlag, T., Nord, I., Beck, W., Bünker, A., Lämmlin, G., Müller, S., Pock, J., & Rothgangel, M. (2023b). Introduction. In T. Schlag, I. Nord, W. Beck, A. Bunker, G. Lämmlein, S. Müller, J. Pock, & M. Rothgangel. (Eds.), *Churches Online in Times of Corona. Die CONTOC-Studie: Empirische Einsichten, Interpretationen und Perspektiven* (pp. 11–17). Wiesbaden: Springer.

Schmidt, E., & Cohen, J. (2013). *The New Digital Age: Transforming Nations, Businesses, and Our Lives*. New York: Vintage.

Scott, S. A. Q. (2016). Algorithmic Absolution: The Case of Catholic Confessional Apps. *Online – Heidelberg Journal of Religions on the Internet*, 11, 254–275.

Serres, M. (2013). *Erfindet euch neu!: Eine Liebeserklärung an die vernetzte Generation*. Berlin: Suhrkamp Verlag.

Sievert, H., & Reimann, R. P. (2021). *Interaktion unerwünscht? Online-Gottesdienste während der Corona-Pandemie. Weitere ausgewählte Ergebnisse der Befragungsstudie „Rezipiententypologie Evangelischer Online-Gottesdienstbesucher*Innen während und nach der Corona-Krise* (SSRN Scholarly Paper No. ID 4029720). Rochester, NY: Social Science Research Network.

Singh, R., & Munderia, R. (2022). Relationship Between Four Needs of Meaning and Smartphone Usage. In A. C.-K. Chan, M. F. Steger, R. C.-F. Chui, N. Y.-F. Siu, S. C. P. Wong Ip, & B. Y.-H. Lam (Eds.), *Proceedings of the Meaning in Life International Conference 2022—Cultivating, Promoting, and Enhancing Meaning in Life Across Cultures and Life Span (MIL 2022)* (pp. 112–125). Dordrecht, The Netherlands: Atlantis Press International BV.

Stalder, F. (2018). *The Digital Condition*. Cambridge/Medford, TX: Polity Press.

Todjeras, P. (2020). Abendmahl feiern in Zeiten der COVID-19-Pandemie. Eine Krise. *Liturgie und Kultur*, 11 (3), 55–83.

Tsuria, R. (2021). Digital Media: When God Becomes Everybody—The Blurring of Sacred and Profane. *Religions*, *12* (2), 1–12.

Tveitereid, K. (2023). Lived Theology and Theology in the Lived. In P. Ward & K. Tveitereid (Eds.), *Wiley Blackwell Companion to Qualitative Research and Theology* (pp. 67–78). Hoboken, NJ: Wiley-Blackwell.

van Dijck, J., & Poell, T. (2013). Understanding Social Media Logic. *Media and Communication*, 1 (1), 2–14.

6 Reclaiming the Equality of Muslim Women in a (Post)digital World

Nuraan Davids

INTRODUCTION

Despite historical accounts of Muslim women actively participating, engaging, and deliberating in early Muslim communities, they are often relegated to marginal and non-agential roles, whether in Muslim-majority, minority or liberal democracies. On the one hand, Muslim women's active and equal involvement in the emergence of Islam in 7th century Arabia is vividly described in the prophetic traditions (Ahmed, 1992; Barlas, 2002; Wadud, 2006). Various accounts reveal Muslim women as actively seeking knowledge alongside men by attending study circles (Ahmed, 1992; Afsaruddin, 2005; Auda, 2017), thereby also bringing into dispute ideas of sexually segregated spaces, that are typically propagated and employed in some contemporary Muslim-based institutions.

On the other hand, the centrality of Muslim women is amplified in the foundational scripture of the Qur'an, which, as Wadud (2002) highlights, contains more passages in relation to women than all other topics combined. Notably, the prominence of women in the Qur'an derives from its response to a profoundly patriarchal-androcentric society. Accepted as the direct word of God, and at once a text of ethical guidance, and a referential framework for all human conduct, the Qur'an is also seen as a reformational revelation in seeking to establish socially just ways of being and acting. Women are explicitly singled out, as the Qur'an promulgates a series of political, social, and economic reform measures, which include women's right to a contract marriage, to inherit, to control their dower and property, as well as provision and protection for widows and orphans, with a specific emphasis on the girl orphan (Qur'an, 4:2–7).

Evidently, however, the centrality afforded to women in both the foundational paradigms of Islam – the Qur'an and the Sunnah (lived example of Prophet Muhammad) – has been largely undermined and often omitted. It is not only that women and their experiences have been excluded from historical and current methods of interpretive reference, contends Wadud (2006), but also that interpretations of the Qur'an in relation to laws, concerning private or public matters, are predominantly based on a male interpretive privilege. As such, normative traditions are typically interpreted in an exclusively male-centric framework and worldview,

DOI: 10.1201/9781003497950-8

including a propagation of males as the only legitimate interpreters of Islam. As will be elaborated upon in the ensuing section, the consequences for Muslim women are far-reaching, not only for their participation in the public and private domains of their faith, but for how they relate and embody their Islamic identity.

Muslim women, in both Muslim-majority and minority contexts, have made some significant strides in countering the patriarchal overbearance which typically seeks to regulate how Muslim women come into and enact their faith. Undoubtedly, these strides have been facilitated by the accessibility of a digital world. Unlike the traditional spaces and structures of Islam, the digital world offers a divergent and subversive space of immediate and endless possibilities, as open to propagating Islam in unprecedented ways, as it is to contesting and disrupting normative ideas and practices of Muslims. To this end, this chapter has a twofold interest. Firstly, to explore the space of a (post)digital world in relation to Islam's paradigmatic foundations, not as textual interpretations, but as lived discourses. Secondly, to consider the role of a (post)digital world in (re)-claiming the Islamic paradigms that centre and equalise the position of women, thereby bringing into question the ethicality of an androcentric belief system.

IMAGING MUSLIM WOMEN

The theological centrality of Muslim women in Islam speaks to her role as the custodian of family values – seen as the cornerstone of a well-functioning society. Their centrality explains why the dominant debates in Islam centre on women's chastity, modesty, inheritance, marriage, education, as well as dress code, and specifically, veiling. The challenge with these debates is that the prioritisation of family life and values by Muslim women is often conflated with confinement to the private sphere of the home, and hence, the construction of Muslim women as fixed domestic entities. This means that notions of modesty, chastity as well as veiling are intimately entangled with seclusion and privacy, thereby problematising their entry and participation in the public sphere (Davids, 2016).

Ironically, the regulation of Muslim women in the public sphere, according to normative Islamic interpretations, is most prominently encountered in mosques, whether in Muslim-majority or minority contexts. It is commonplace for Muslims to establish a mosque wherever they find themselves, signalling the core role of the mosque not only as a place of worship but as a collective and communal space of gathering, which often extends into an array of social, educational, and cultural services. In Muslim-minority contexts in which Muslims might experience marginalisation and even antagonism, mosques often provide a sense of inclusion, belonging, and safety (Davids, 2023). Critical to the establishment of mosques is a recognition that they belong to and are exclusively for the worship of God (Qur'an, 72, p.18). I highlight this recognition because it provides a contradictory perspective on how mosques are often deployed as an exclusively male domain.

There are numerous accounts of mosques being deployed as gendered spaces (Lewicki and O'Toole, 2017; Nyhagen, 2019; Nas, 2021), with the presence of women not only considered as a physical intrusion, but also censured as sacrilegious (Hoel, 2013; Nyhagen, 2019). The prohibition of access to Muslim women does not have to be expressly articulated by mosque (male) committees; exclusionary measures can take on more subtle forms of inadequate provision of prayer space, or ablution facilities (Sherwood, 2018; Aly, 2018; Alyanak, 2019). Likewise, curricula or teachings in Muslim-majority societies do not have to be explicitly gender discriminatory, rather, as Shah and Iqbal (2011) observe, the discourses that have been produced and legitimised in the name of religion are often gendered.

Importantly, the practices depicted here are not reflective of historical accounts of the first Muslim community, where, according to Esposito and DeLong-Bas (2001), women prayed in mosques unsegregated from men, were involved in hadith transmission, engaged in commercial transactions, and were encouraged to seek and share knowledge. Any prohibition of women from the mosque would have been made evident by Islam's paradigmatic source codes. Yet, most Muslim women do not contest their exclusion or marginalisation. There are at least two possible reasons for their silence. One centres on the pervasiveness of conservative views and interpretations of Islam in Muslim-majority countries, which, states Abusharaf (2006), often translates into a politics of exclusion for women. This politics of exclusion extends beyond access to mosques and includes an entrenched social discourse intent upon mobilising control over all public activities of Muslim women, such as her right to education, working and travelling unaccompanied by a male guardian (Abusharaf, 2006). Similar discourses are prevalent in Muslim-minority societies, explains Sahin (2018), where immigrant communities have transplanted and reproduced educational and social practices from their home countries, so that they might retain religious and cultural connections.

The second reason, which feeds into the first, is that although 'Muslim women directly experience the consequences of oppressive misreadings of religious texts, few question their legitimacy, and fewer still have explored the liberatory aspects of the Qur'an's teachings' (Barlas, 2002, p. 3). To Barlas (2001), the neglect in understanding the Qur'an as a historical text, and engaging with its content, has contributed to the failure of reading, and understanding the Qur'an as a complex hermeneutic totality. This begins to explain, on the one hand, why some men might perpetuate gender inequalities, and on the other hand, why some women might unquestionably accept and normalise their subjugated roles and reproduce their own discrimination (Abusharaf, 2006).

Notably, the same centrality assigned to Muslim women in Islam is also found in some liberal democracies, albeit for different reasons (Davids, 2020). The debates within Islam focus on women in relation to their modesty, chastity and piety, and hence, as an embodiment and preservation of Islamic values. The debates in liberal democracies, however, are directed at dis-embodying Muslim women from their Islamic identities by regulating and prohibiting their right to veil or wear a hijab (Davids, 2020). Muslim women, explains Bilge (2010), are simultaneously and illogically depicted as victims of an oppressive, patriarchal religion, and as threat to the way of life and freedom of Western modernity. Of course, these discourses are not new constructions. Setting Muslim women as a de facto oppressed group because they are presumably 'forced' to wear a veil or hijab, bodes well for the extension colonialist narrative as emancipator. This, despite the reality that Muslim women are neither defined by a common identity, nor by a common understanding of Qur'anic exegeses. Women are motivated by different reasons for veiling, which, on the one hand, includes religious compliance, personal piety, and family and societal pressure (Kirmani, 2009), and on the other hand, as expressions of identity, cultural or political assertion, solidarity and resistance (Golnaraghi & Dye, 2016). Muslim women's persistence, however, in wearing the veil is seen as a resistance to a liberal way of life.

It is not only a matter of liberal democracies conceiving themselves as the benchmarks of freedom and modernisation, but also that this benchmark is dyadically contingent on the construction of a backward 'Other' (Kirmani, 2009). Hence, interpretations of Muslim women as sexually constrained, ignorant, poor, uneducated, tradition bound, religious, domesticated and victimised are juxtaposed against the portrayal of Western women as educated, modern, liberated, and in control over their bodies (Mohanty, 1988). In this way, Muslim women are recast as symbolic images, fundamentally at odds with 'western values', thereby sustaining a binary between the Orient and the Occident. Of greater concern is that the deployment of female Muslim bodies as 'symbolic confrontations between a re-essentialized understanding of religious and cultural differences and the forces of state power' (Benhabib, 2011, p. 168), holds immensely complex implications for Muslim women. In highlighting the trend of gendered Islamophobia, Akel (2021) reports that 70% of Islamophobic hate speech and acts in France were directed at women; during 2017, 56% of victims of Islamophobia in the UK were women, citing that they were more likely to be attacked if seen wearing distinctly Islamic garments (Akel, 2021). Muslim women, contends Petzen (2012), are becoming increasingly stigmatised, criminalised and marked for social and economic exclusion.

Thus far, I have provided some insights into the symbolic imaging and lived experiences of Muslim women both within their faith communities and outside of it. By drawing attention to their theological centrality in Islam, as well as their political centrality in liberal democracies, have also revealed their vulnerability, unequal treatment and marginalisation. In the second half of this chapter, I turn my attention to the potential role of a (post)digital world in (re)-claiming the equality of Muslim women and bringing into question the ethicality of an androcentric belief system.

REAPPROPRIATING IMAGES AND MEANING IN A 'THIRD SPACE'

Following the above discussion, it becomes apparent that contemporary interpretations and responses to Muslim women, whether from within or outside of their faith communities, coincide in approaching these women as non-agential – meaning that they are incapable of thinking, acting or actively influencing any decision. It might indeed be the case in some instances, that Muslim women have relinquished their own power and autonomy by neglecting to engage with the Qur'an as a historical text and as a complex hermeneutic totality (Barlas, 2001). However, it is also the case that some Muslim women are intentionally constructing a spaceless zone, out of the reach of normative textuality and political rhetoric. This zone is reminiscent of Bhabha's (1994, p. 37) third space, which, although unrepresentable in itself, constitutes 'the discursive conditions of enunciation that ensure that the meaning and symbols of culture have no primordial unity or fixity; that even the same signs can be appropriated, translated, rehistoricised and read anew'.

Devoid of geography, location, time, boundaries, or binaries, like many other communities – whether centric or liminal – Muslim women are turning to the digital world as a 'third space' not only as a convergence of religious identity, but perhaps more importantly, as a space for re-interrogating, re-establishing, and reclaiming their purpose, meaning, and authority beyond the reach of normative interference and imposition. For Bhabha (1994), 'the beyond' opens new possibilities of thinking, being and acting. This is because 'there is a sense of disorientation, a disturbance of direction, in the 'beyond': an exploratory, restless movement' (Bhabha, 1994, p. 1). It is as much an unfamiliar space of dissent and contestation, as it is fluid and comfortable – not only in terms of the content of deliberations and debates, but also in terms of who has claimed the right to speak.

Traditionally, explain Bouziane et al. (2022), religious teachings are a reserved domain for a group of male professionals, who communicate and propagate Islam in ritualised forms and in formalised contexts. In some instances, these same men have transferred the same type of knowledge, which they acquired through their traditional education and clerical training onto digital platforms (Bouziane et al., 2022). Some Islamic religious leaders advise their followers not to use social media platforms. However, according to Ibahrine (2014), most scholars and preachers, capitalise on the effectiveness and efficiency of social media in engaging with the community of believers and enhancing their fidelity and loyalty. In most cases, however, digital platforms have empowered a new generation of social media influencers, individuals and communities to re-negotiate entrenched understandings of religion and authority, thereby subverting the often assumed closedness of religious and cultural systems within Muslim societies (Bouziane et al., 2022). Nisa (2019) contends that digital platforms have led to an increased fragmentation of authority in Islam, so that Islamic discourses are no longer monopolised by religious elites or *ulama*, especially male elites.

To Bouziane et al. (2022, p. 2), these individuals are not only adept in digital media production, but they also hold a cosmopolitan worldview, 'whose religious practice focuses on storytelling rather than dogmatic texts, on human relationships, civil life, and what it means to be and act as a human being who happens to be a Muslim'. Hence, Bunt's (2018) argument is that although social media disrupts and relativises traditional religious hierarchies, there is no ideological uniformity to be found in cyber-Islamic environments. Instead, the digitisation of Islam and Muslims adopt and fulfil an array of formats and functions. On the one hand, it includes dogmatic, as well as liberal and feminist views. On the other hand, states Ibahrine (2014), social media have become the ideal platform, the new mosque or madrasa for the dissemination of the Islamic belief; social media have also become integrated in the habit of not only proselytising Islam, but also safeguarding Islam against critics from the outside.

MUSLIM WOMEN: RECLAIMING THEIR VOICE AND AGENCY

For Muslim women, says Islam (2019), the advent of social media platforms has brought about a unique space where Muslim women are engaging in new forms of resistive practices, which includes, reshaping discourses around female identity, agency, autonomy, as well as advocating for social change. Moreover, these women are not only from the west, but from a cross-spectrum of geographical locations and cultural identities – putting into practice new formations of a Muslim *ummah* [community]. These women, states Islam (2019, p. 229), are using digital spaces 'to supplement their offline subjectivities as agentic actors and engage with a variety of communities to transform their lived realities'. Hence, we find, says Nisa (2019), diverse cyberactivism expressions, which include those who use social media platforms to voice their concerns regarding gender inequality, as well as those who use it to accentuate their versions of true expressions of Islam. To Nisa (2019), the digital environment has boosted the presence of the voices of these women, that reflect diverse, segmented, and fragmented Islamic public spheres.

Social media campaigns and projects, for example, have challenged the gendered use of mosques, often allocating women inadequate ablution and prayer facilities (Sherwood, 2018; Aly, 2018; Alyanak, 2019). Ironically, some mosques in the UK, for example, are happy to open their doors to the public in efforts to boost community relations (Aly, 2018), but are unwilling to provide 'spatial equality' for women (Alyanak, 2019). Advocating for spatial and gender equality, as captured in 'Women in mosques' campaigns, whether in the UK, Scotland, Turkey, Egypt, Australia or South Africa, are not progressive calls. Instead, it is an appeal for a regression to the experiences of the first Muslim community, in which women were actively involved and participated in forging their religious identities and establishing a new faith community.

Calls for a return to the ways of life during the historical unfolding of Islam are not limited to access and participation in mosques. Considering the growing antagonism against the wearing of the hijab in liberal societies, making it increasingly difficult for Muslim women to access and participate in these spaces, this type of relegation forces women to seek alternative spaces of safety, inclusion and belonging. Here, the digital space brings together not only Muslim women within particular societies, but also across diasporic communities, sharing common subjections to surveillance and regulation. By sharing their stories, states Islam (2019), they might empower themselves as well as other Muslim women by resisting controlling images that seek to misrepresent them in Western visual media.

In turn, Muslim women in Indonesia – home to Islam's largest Muslim population – use digital platforms as a 'feminist counter-voice, particularly Islamic feminism, to encode alternative narratives and demystify meaning-making processes related to polygamy and issues of sexual violence in Indonesia' (Rifani & Tambunan, 2021, p. 53). Sreberny (2015) explains that while much of the online activity in Muslim-majority contexts has a national origin and focus, and is conducted in regional languages such as Arabic, Persian, and Turkish, a great deal of material is also shared in English and French, with several sites providing links to other campaigns and events happening elsewhere, addressing transnational feminist sympathies. Additionally, it is evident, continues Sreberny (2015), that much of this online activity is conducted and aided by what can be broadly termed 'Middle East diasporas' in Europe, the United States, and elsewhere. By blurring the geopolitical boundaries between the inside and outside of national spaces, digital technology facilitates the emergence of transnational interconnections between women in the region and beyond (Sreberny, 2015).

By lifting their voices on digital platforms, Muslim women are debunking the myths of their essentialised oppression and contesting their placement as the proverbial and irreconcilable 'Other' (Islam, 2019). Beyond the myths and displacement of the public square – whether in Muslim-majority or liberal-democratic societies – digital spaces are not only without constraint and restraint. Despite the intangibility of its cyber characterisation, which alludes to 'a sense of disorientation, an exploratory, restless movement' (Bhabha, 1994, p. 1), digital spaces are the literal in-between spaces through which Muslim women can break free from their misrepresentation and marginalisation. In this way, argues Islam (2019, p. 230), digital spaces 'can become crucial, transformative spaces where Muslim women might resist culturally reinforced and institutionalized knowledge'. In the concluding discussion I turn my attention to the potential role of a (post)digital world in (re)-claiming the equality of Muslim women and bring into question the ethicality of an androcentric belief system.

(RE)-CLAIMING THE EQUALITY OF MUSLIM WOMEN IN A (POST-DIGITAL) WORLD

In the previous section I highlighted that in some instances, such as Muslim women calling for spatial equality in mosques, these calls can be understood as a mobilisation towards the ways things were during the historical emergence of Islam, rather than new and progressive thinking. Similar arguments can be made in relation to gender equality and justice, which include matters of marriage, divorce, and women being seen and treated as autonomous beings. Even the increasing deployment of Muslim women's bodies as sites of 'symbolic confrontations' between a re-essentialized understanding of religious and cultural differences expression and the forces of state power' (Benhabib, 2011, p. 168) are not new, but an extension of the colonialist fixation with the veil or hijab.

The point is, that other than 'the state of exception', which, according to Santos (2007, p. 16), 'restricts democratic rights under the guise of safeguarding or even expanding them' – as is evident in the prohibition of the hijab in public domains, such as schools – none of the dominant debates by or on Muslim women, can be classified as new. By implication, this means that Muslim women and how they choose to express their Islamic identities, regardless or because of socio-political contexts have always been under scrutiny and subjected to public debate. Hence, the Qur'an's promulgation of far-reaching changes to the personal and social conditions of Muslim women. There are more passages in the Qur'an, states with Wadud (2002), that address issues pertaining to women, as individuals, as part of a family and, as members of a community, than all the other issues combined.

Few can disagree that the digital space has facilitated a dual process of disrupting stereotypes, while empowering Muslim women to take ownership of how their identities are constructed, bringing into disrepute normative ideas of Muslim women as a homogenous and oppressed entity. Certainly, contends Hirji (2021), the Internet has given voice and helped to amplify those who would otherwise be silenced, or who would not have the same reach when voicing the same opinions in real life. The articulation of alternative voices, interpretations and perspectives, can bring into question certain dogmas and practices. However, this should not be confused, with eradicating deeply entrenched tropes regarding Muslim women, or erasing the restrictions that society places on Muslim women (Hirji, 2021). Hirji (2021, p. 81) cautions that groups, that are vulnerable to harassment in real life, are also vulnerable online:

> For women, especially women of color and/or Muslim women or women whose identity is Othered, cyberspace is not a neutral or safe space. It carries some of the same entanglements, contradictions, and injustices as the so-called real world.

Whatever inequalities Muslim women experience – whether in the privacy of their homes, or the public spaces of work or the mosque – will persist and might even intensify in response to women's activism. The digital space is not only used by dissenting or protesting voices. It is also used by those, who wish to push back against reform, who wish to preserve their status quo, and who sees any calls for change not as a criticism on a particular practice or organisation, but as an attack on the system or religion. Hence, when Muslim women asks for spatial equality in mosques, they are seen as stepping out of line and acting contrary to Islam. When Muslim men provide a counter-response to 'women-in-mosques' campaigns, they do not offer these responses as individuals, or mosque committees. Instead, they rely on androcentric interpretations of Islam, not only to discount the call, but also to bring into disrepute the belief and character of the protesting women. They do this, because it is easier to discredit women, than it is to justify a view, which in the end, might not be justifiable. One should not, therefore, underestimate the difficulties Muslim women might encounter when they move out of the digital space and into the real world (Hirji, 2021).

The digital space can be an immensely liberating forum, bolstered and supported by an array of like-minded individuals and organisations, which can effect meaningful change in this world. The digital space has already shown what is possible when Muslim women are mobilised and take control of their own narratives. Like the digital classroom which can provide greater inclusion and participation, by ensuring the anonymity of students, the digital space can provide a 'protective screen', which affords agency and autonomy, which some Muslim women might not have in the real spaces and encounters of their lives. The framing of a screen creates a certain detached anonymity, and hence, a perceived measure of safety. Stated differently, deliberating on matters in a space which is 'safe' even when there are push-backs or harassment, is unlike physical spaces where the hijab, and hence, Muslim women, are perceivably cause for regulation, suspicion, or exclusion. By engaging with others on digital platforms, it is possible to begin to see the world from their perspectives and recognise that these multiple perspectives and truths actually exist.

Through our imagination, explains Nussbaum (2006, p. 8),

> we are able to have a kind of insight into the experience of another group or person that it is very difficult to attain in daily life—particularly when our world has constructed sharp separations between groups, and suspicions that make any encounter difficult.

Inasmuch, therefore, as the digital space allows for the reappropriation and reinterpretation of signs (Bhabha, 1994), there are irretractable tensions between re-clarifying signs or images in a digital world, and how these signs are interpreted and deployed in the real world. We might be able to acknowledge, theoretically and in conversation, that racism, sexism, and Islamophobia are wrong, but that does not mean that our attitudes towards 'black', Muslim women will necessarily be less prejudicial. There are debates and discussions that are both plausible and logical within liminal spaces, or spaces beyond the reach of contextual climate and politics. Although digital technology has the capacity to amplify and connect voices and perspectives in ways that could be of tremendous benefit to society, generally, that same capacity cannot replace our human need for equality and inclusion.

It seems natural, therefore, to consider other avenues of engagement, which is as porous as it is human. In this regard, a postdigital space holds appeal in that it accepts the pervasive presence and importance of a digital world; it recognises the alternativity of this space which can transcend certain debates in ways that are just not possible in real time and place. However, a postdigital world also recognises the loss of intimacy and human connection that comes with communicating in a liminal space. We have intense connectivity but less human connection, and this scenario is not without risks to individuals, communities or campaigns. These risks are not limited to potential online backlash, or harassment. Instead, the risks include mistakenly believing that digital debates and support can naturally flow into the physical world. These two worlds might be connected, but they are also separate. A postdigital world recognises that what connects these two worlds is in fact, humans, and what remains beyond digital engagement, are the lived realities of people.

The tensions which Muslim women encounter within their faith communities and outside in liberal democracies can be deliberated upon, but they cannot be resolved in a digital space. Garnering 'likes' and support for a particular view, does not translate into a less androcentric public space, or a more democratic society than what is currently on offer in some liberal democracies. The equality which most Muslim women seek is abundantly evident in the source codes of Islam: the Qur'an and the *Sunnah* [lived examples of Prophet Muhammad]. All Muslim women have to do to liberate themselves from marginalisation, oppression and exclusion within their faith communities is to directly engage with these codes and to follow these engagements with real-life action into spaces from which they might be prohibited, such as mosques. Until Muslim women enact the liberatory discourses which are already at their disposal, they will neither be able to contest their relegation nor will they be able to disrupt the propensity of an androcentric interpretation as the only interpretation of Islam. I see this as a critical point, because it calls for action beyond digital sharing, and it necessitates a physical embodiment of the equality being not only demanded but also assumed.

The same argument pertains to the antagonisms seemingly provoked by the hijab in some liberal democracies. Here I need to pause to clarify that I am not implying that Muslim women are not already acting and taking physical control of their bodies and how they access the public sphere. What I am arguing for is a deeper understanding of the source codes that can unfold with direct engagement with the text and in relation to others. Presumptions in some liberal democracies that Muslim women who wear a hijab do so not out of choice, but due to coercion from male relatives, infers that either Muslim women do not have agency, or that they do not voluntarily choose to wear a hijab. Both perspectives reveal an impoverished understanding of Muslim women, of their faith, and of the hijab. To alter this understanding requires an unlearning of biases pertaining to Muslim women. It also requires a learning about Islam. Neither Muslim women, or any other faith community, nor religions exist in a digital space. Both are shaped in human traditions and interactions. They are influenced by language, cultural discourses, geographical locations, and social values. The unlearning, therefore, of misinterpretations and misunderstandings can only happen through human engagement and the re-establishment of relationships, which are fundamental to nurturing empathy and compassion. In the end, the perceived voicelessness of Muslim women can only be disrupted in real time and space, not only by assuming but also by (re)-claiming their own equality.

REFERENCES

Abusharaf, A. (2006). Women in Islamic Communities: The Quest for Gender Justice Research. *Human Rights Quarterly*, 28(3), 714–728. doi:10.1353/hrq.2006.0027.

Afsaruddin, A. (2005). Muslim Views on Education: Parameters, Purview, and Possibilities. *Journal of Catholic Legal Studies*, 44(143), 143–178.

Ahmed, L. (1992). *Women and Gender in Islam: Historical Roots of a Modern Debate*. New Haven, CT: Yale University Press.

Akel, S. (2021). *Institutionalised: The Rise of Islamophobia in Higher Education*. Project Report. London Metropolitan University. Retrieved February, 2, 2024, from https://repository.londonmet.ac.uk/6295/

Aly, R. (2018). UK Mosques Must Make Space for Women – Not Turn Us Away. Retrieved February 2, 2024, from https://www.theguardian.com/commentisfree/2018/feb/19/british-muslim-women-open-mosque-initiative

Alyanak, O. (2019). When Women Demand Prayer Space: Women in Mosques Campaign in Turkey. *Journal of Middle East Women's Studies*, 15(1), 125–134.

Auda, J. (2017). *Reclaiming the Mosque: The Role of Women in Islam's House of Worship*. Swansea: Claritas Books.

Barlas, A. (2001). The Qur'an and Hermeneutics: Reading the Qur'an's Opposition to Patriarchy. *Journal of Qur'anic Studies*, 3(2), 15–38.

Barlas, A. (2002). *Believing Women in Islam: Unreading Patriarchal Interpretations of the Qur'an*. Austin: University of Texas Press.

Bhabha, H. K. (1994). *The Location of Culture*. London: Routledge.

Benhabib, S. (2011). *Dignity in Adversity: Human Rights in Troubled Times*. Oxford, UK: Oxford University Press.

Bilge, S. (2010). Beyond Subordination vs. Resistance: An Intersectional Approach to the Agency of Veiled Muslim Women. *Journal of Intercultural Studies*, 31(1), 9–28.

Bouziane, Z., Fedtke, J., Shin, D. D., El Kadoussi, A., & Ibahrine, M. (2022). Digital Islam and Muslim Millennials: How Social Media Influencers Reimagine Religious Authority and Islamic Practices. *Religions*, 13, 335. doi:10.3390/rel13040335

Bunt, G. R. (2018). *Hashtag Islam: How Cyber-Islamic Environments Are Transforming Religious Authority*. Chapel Hill: The University of North Carolina Press.

Davids, N. (2016). Religion, Culture, and the Exclusion of Muslim Women: On Finding a Reimagined form of Inclusive-Belonging. *Knowledge Cultures,* 4(4), 46–59.

Davids, N. (2020). The Controversy of Muslim Women in Liberal Democracies. In K. Hytten (Ed.), *The Oxford Encyclopedia of Philosophy of Education* (pp. 1–19). New York: Oxford University Press.

Davids, N. (2023). An Educational Opportunity for (Re)-Scripting Gender Justice as an Imperative of Faith and Citizenship: A South African Case. *British Journal of Religious Education,* 45(2), 162–171.

Esposito, J. L. & DeLong-Bas, N. (2001). *Women in Muslim Family Law.* Syracuse: Syracuse University Press.

Golnaraghi, G., & Dye, K. (2016). Discourses of Contradiction: A Postcolonial Analysis of Muslim Women and the Veil. *International Journal of Cross Cultural Management,* 16(2), 137–152.

Hirji, F. (2021). Claiming Our Space: Muslim Women, Activism, and Social Media. *Islamophobia Studies Journal*, 6(1), 78–92.

Hoel, N. 2013. "Feminism and Religion and the Politics of Location: Situating Islamic Feminism in South Africa," *Journal of Gender and Religion in Africa, 19* (2), 73–89.

Ibahrine, M. (2014). Islam and Social Media. In H. Kerric (Ed.), *Encyclopedia of Social Media and Politics* (pp. 736–740). London: SAGE.

Islam, I (2019). Virginia Tech Redefining #YourAverageMuslim Woman: Muslim Female Digital Activism on Social Media. *Journal of Arab & Muslim Media Research,* 12(2), 213–233.

Kirmani, N. (2009). Deconstructing and Reconstructing "Muslim Women" through Women's Narratives. *Journal of Gender Studies*, 18(1), 47–62.

Lewicki, A., & O'Toole, T. (2017. Acts and Practices of Citizenship: Muslim Women's Activism in the UK. *Ethnic and Racial Studies,* 40(1), 152–171. doi:10.1080/01419870.2016.1216142.

Mohanty, C. (1988). Under Western Eyes: Feminist Scholarship and Colonial Discourses. *Feminist Review,* 30, 65–88.

Nas, A. (2021). 'Women in Mosques': Mapping the Gendered Religious Space through Online Activism. *Feminist Media Studies,* 1(1), 11–43. doi:10.1080/14680777.2021.1878547.170.

Nisa, E. F. (2019). Internet and Muslim Women. In M. Woodward & R. Lukens-Bull (Eds.), *Handbook of Contemporary Islam and Muslim Lives* (pp. 1023–1042). Cham: Springer. doi:10.1007/978-3-319-73653-2_71-1.

Nussbaum, M. (2006). *Education for Democratic Citizenship.* Lecture at the Institute of Social Studies, The Hague, The Netherlands, 9 March. Retrieved March, 12, from chrome-extension://efaidnbmnnnibpcajpcglclefindmkaj/https://www.eur.nl/sites/corporate/files/nussbaum_text.pdf

Nyhagen, L. (2019). Mosques as Gendered Spaces: The Complexity of Women's Compliance with, and Resistance to, Dominant Gender Norms, and the Importance of Male Allies. *Religions*, 10(321), 1–15. doi:10.3390/rel10050321.

Petzen, J. (2012). Contesting Europe: A Call for an Anti-Modern Sexual Politics. *European Journal of Women's Studies,* 19(1), 97–114.

Rifani, A. N., & Tambunan, S. M. G. (2021). Media Activism: Reinterpretation Digital Sisterhood by @mubadalah.id, @muslimahfeminis, @cherbonfeminist on Social Media Instagram in Indonesia. *Advances in Social Science, Education and Humanities Research,* 593, 52–60.

Sahin, A. (2018). Critical Issues in Islamic Education Studies: Rethinking Islamic and Western Liberal Secular Values of Education. *Religions*, 9(11), 329–335. doi:10.3390/rel9110335.

Santos, B. D. (2007). Beyond Abyssal Thinking: From Global Lines to Ecologies of Knowledges. *Review*, 30(1), 45–89.

Shah, S., & Iqbal, M. (2011). Pakistani Diaspora in Britain: Intersections of Multi-Locationality and Girls' Education. *British Journal of Sociology of Education*, 32(5), 763–783. doi:10.1080/01425692.2011.596376.

Sherwood, H. (2018). Muslim Women Call for More Equality in Running UK Mosques. Retrieved, March, 12, from https://www.theguardian.com/uk-news/2018/aug/18/uk-muslim-women-call-for-more-equality-mosques.

Sreberny, A. (2015). Women's Digital Activism in a Changing Middle East. *International Journal of Middle East Studies,* 47, 357–361.

Wadud, A. (2002) A'ishah's Legacy. *New Internationalist Magazine*, 345(1).

Wadud, A. (2006). *Inside the Gender Jihad: Women's Reform in Islam.* Oxford: Oneworld Publications.

Part III

Theoretical Debates

7 The Commons: Enclosures or Thresholds?

John Reader and Maria Power

> And fear came upon every soul: and many wonders and signs were done among the apostles. And all who believed were together and had all things in common; and they sold their possessions and goods and distributed them to all, as any had need.
>
> *(Acts 2:43–45)*

What do we mean by 'The Commons'? We have probably encountered it in terms such as "the Common Good"; "the Commonwealth", or even The House of Commons. Although these are related, they are not quite the same. I tried the term out with our 14-year-old grandson to see what he made of it on the basis that you need to ask a teenager while they still know everything. We quickly got into a discussion about water as something that should or might be freely accessible for all as we need this to live – not the case in some parts of the world where access is through payment only. He then talked about the NHS – another controversial area but one where I would agree with him that under the Welfare State as originally designed health care was supposedly free to all at the point of access. Energy seemed to be another similar area as we rely on this to function whether through food or electricity for instance. Then we got onto discussion about the internet and he suggested that through Mr Google we had access to all the knowledge in the world. I raised the point that Google is only one search engine that determines what we might find through its own algorithms and Page Rank system so that is not quite so clear cut. Hopefully you begin to get the general picture now. What are those resources or things that we might hold in common or should be held in common, and, if they aren't, need to be the subject of political challenge?

Why enclosures and thresholds though? A quick dive into history informs us that most large estates and land holdings have been created by enclosures of 'the Commons'; ways in which violence was often used to appropriate land from others in order to construct such estates. Think about the Highland Clearances for instance. From an economic perspective one could say that this is about the imposition of a particular distribution of a scarce and finite resource. Yet this is not so obviously the case when it comes to the internet as my grandson has a point that everything is potentially available if you know how and where to search. This too however has been enclosed by the Big Tech companies for their own financial advantage and most

DOI: 10.1201/9781003497950-10

of us collude with their power for the sake of convenience. We accept enclosures as the way things normally work even though some will inevitably lose out. Thresholds could either be attempts to create new commons or to protect existing ones through protest and political challenge: ways through to a more just and equitable distribution or means of access to whatever it might be. So how far can this concept take us as we strive for a better world?

An early forerunner in the consideration of this was Aldo Leopold and his proposal for a Land Ethic (1970/1949). His idea was that ethics should be expanded to include our relationship to the land, and indeed to animals, plants, soils and waters. The impact of this would be to change the role of *Homo sapiens* from that of conqueror of the land to that of a plain member and citizen of it. This would imply respect for one's fellow members both human and non-human and thus for the whole ecological community. Land use should cease to not only be seen as solely an economic problem but also be viewed in ethical and aesthetical terms.

Although this feels like a step in the right direction, I discovered that this is not far enough for many. Northcott in *A Political Theology of Climate Change* (2014) describes how contemporary environmental philosophers such as Callicott (2013) argue that this still operates within an Enlightenment understanding of the relationship between the human and nature and relies on a dualistic approach where human domination and the separation of the material from the spiritual is still in play (p. 301). Leopold (19does talk about the idea of a pyramid suggesting a hierarchy with humans at the top. The question of whether the wider concept of the Commons is still too anthropocentric is an important one to bear in mind.

As an aside, if you want to track down land ownership in the UK a good source is Guy Shrubsole's *Who Owns England?* (2019). From the best available figures in September 2018 his appendices give chapter and verse on both public and privately owned land (p. 296ff). He concludes that: "England as a whole belongs to a tiny number of people and organisations. Just 36,000 landowners – a mere 0.06% of the population – own half of the rural land in England and Wales" (p. 21). This is according to the Country Land and Business Association who represent the land lobby in Westminster. "Many of England's largest landowners have acquired their land through inheritance; an inheritance that has often been built on the back of conquest and enclosure" (p. 22). The personnel might change over time but the basic structure of land ownership has survived for generations. This of course has environmental consequences. So much for 'the Commons' then in terms of land!

You will not be surprised to learn that such revelations lead easily into more radical political ideas although the ones I will share come from a more US-based source. In their book "Commonwealth" (2009) the political philosophers Hardt and Negri develop the concept in greater detail.

At the time they were responding to the impacts of the global financial crisis and that is why I became interested in their ideas, but revisiting this they still seem relevant. In their view, The Common means the common wealth of the material world: air, water, fruits of the soil; plus also the result of social production, knowledges, languages, codes, information, affects. Their focus is on practices of interaction, care and co-habitation in a common world, promoting the beneficial and limiting the detrimental forms of the common. Their basic argument is that neo-liberal regimes seek to privatise the common, turning cultural products into private property. This is to be resisted.

What they are doing is to bring together concerns for the environmental and the digital, hence their references to knowledge, codes and information. Given the developments in artificial intelligence (AI) and the increased prevalence of digital technology in all our lives, this seems even more important to grasp than it did in 2009. An annoying example for dinosaurs such as myself is public car parking which is now largely controlled by companies such as RingGo which require that one downloads their app in order to be able to book a parking space. I realise that this both simplifies and cuts costs – and removes people from the process – but this is imposed and becomes yet another enclosure in my opinion. To participate in normal life, one is being forced to go digital without any thought as to the consequences of this both for privacy and employment. Covid of course has accelerated this process or been used as the occasion to do so.

Hardt and Negri are concerned about issues of social justice and talk about the party of the poor and those who have no right to be counted according to current power regimes. Another example perhaps of what we now call the digital divide. In almost theological terms they argue for a "new patristic". When the intellectual is charged with the task of not only denouncing error and unmasking illusions, but also to produce a new truth.

This would put rationality at the service of life; technique at the service of ecological needs; and the accumulation of wealth at the service of the common. All this is to be grounded in the terrain of collective practice through strategic investigation, a form of militancy.

Economists tend to talk in terms of externalities and internalities. So, there are negative externalities such as air pollution; traffic congestion; noisy neighbours; high crime rates, and then the positive ones such as proximity to playgrounds and open space; a dynamic local culture; intellectual circuits of exchange; peaceful and stimulating social interactions. In these we see a spectre of the common, but they are not financially or economically quantifiable and do not obey "market rules". By contrast again in theological language they advocate an Exodus, so reappropriating the common, taking back what is ours.

Finally, Hardt and Negri argue the need to keep "the common" and "the public" conceptually separate. The common exists on a different plane from the private and the public and is fundamentally autonomous from both. The common in both its natural and artificial forms is becoming the central and essential element in all sectors of economic production. Rather than seeing the common in the form of externalities or "missing markets" or "market failures", we should instead see private property in terms of the "missing common" and "common failures". Hence, they use the concept as a means of identifying the enclosures of the Commons but also as a way of forging new thresholds either by protecting existing commons or creating new ones.

This concept is also to be encountered in Kate Raworth's *Doughnut Economics* (2022). The doughnut is defined thus:

> Humanity's 21st century challenge is to meet the needs of all within the means of the planet. In other words, to ensure that no one falls short on life's essentials (from food and housing to healthcare and political voice), while ensuring that collectively we do

> not overshoot our pressure on Earth's life-supporting systems, on which we fundamentally depend – such as a stable climate, fertile soils, and a protective ozone layer. The Doughnut of social and planetary boundaries is a playfully serious approach to framing that challenge, and it acts as a compass for human progress this century.

In a key section of the book, she raises the following questions in relation to the issues of design and distribution (pp. 178–198). Who owns the land? Who makes your money? Who owns your labour? Who will own the robots and then who owns the ideas?

THE DOUGHNUT OF SOCIAL AND PLANETARY BOUNDARIES (2017)

Having registered that land enclosures have been taking place over a long period of time, Raworth argues that this is taking place again today with renewed international investor interest triggered by the 2007–2008 global food crisis (p. 180). Since 2000, foreign investors have made 1,200 large-scale land deals in low and middle-income countries acquiring more than 43 million hectares of land – an area bigger than Japan. Very often these have been land grabs accompanied by promises that have not been fulfilled. So, communities have found themselves dispossessed, dispersed and impoverished.

This exercise of so-called market forces at work is sometimes backed up with reference to Hardin's work which is why this is important to note and understand. In the article, *Science* in 1968, Hardin coined the phrase "the Tragedy of the Commons" which is the most likely phrase you will hear in relation to this subject. He argues that opening common land up to everyone will lead to degradation, free-loading and exploitation of this scarce resource. So, if a pasture is made available in this way, each herder will add more and more animals at the expense of both other herders and the pasture itself. Effectively, every man (or woman) for themselves. Aristotle said something similar: "what is common to the greatest number has the least care bestowed on it". The idea of everyone respecting a "common interest" and designing a system that benefits all is pure idealism. Hence the tragedy.

This was subsequently challenged by research carried out and published in "Governing the Commons" by Elinor Ostrom (1990, 1992) for which she won a Nobel prize in economics. Raworth concludes:

> Gathering a rich array of case studies of 'common-pool' resource users, from Southern India to Southern California, she and her colleagues analysed how diverse communities had, sometimes for generations, successfully collaborated in harvesting, stewarding, and sustaining forests, fishing grounds and waterways.
>
> *(p. 181)*

I have to say that I would be more cautious than this. The examples are not that diverse, and some are certainly historical, and when this does work it tends to be in small scale and containable areas. I think the challenge is to show that respecting the Commons and implementing appropriate monitoring of them can be scaled up and applied to the digital as well as the environment. The respective contributions of Hardin and Ostrom are, however, the ones that get referred to in the wider economic debates.

What Raworth draws out of the debate is that it is possible to provide evidence of distributions of the Commons which are not reliant on market forces, but rather on agreement and consensus by the parties themselves in such a way as to create more equitable systems which are kinder on the environment. She does add though that even Ostrom did not suggest that a one-size fits all model of managing land could be a solution, neither the market, the Commons or the state. "Approaches to distributive land design must fit the people and the place, and may well work best when they combine all three of these approaches to provisioning" (p. 182). In other words, doing things differently is possible and the concept of the Commons may be one component of such processes.

Having now looked at the most obvious example of the Commons from an environmental perspective, I want to turn to some different examples to see whether the concept is of relevance to them. The first of these is the realm of the digital where it is not so clear cut whether we are dealing with a finite or infinite resource.

Susskind and Susskind, in their recent book *The Future of the Professions* (updated edition 2022 OUP), raise the question of the extent to which developments in AI are likely to have a detrimental impact upon the future of medics; educationalists; lawyers; accountants; management consultants and even clergy! Now that so much more information is available to the lay person through the internet, what is the role of such professionals in the coming years?

The key question is that of how we share expertise in society (p. 3). We tend to assume that professionals have knowledge, experience, skills and know-how that those they help do not (p. 5). The critique of professionals is that they are elitist; unaffordable and hide behind specialist jargon in order to protect their status (p. 16). It is increasingly the case that only the rich or robustly insured can engage many top-flight professionals so the expertise of the few is being bestowed upon a few (p. 42). This leads to two questions: how well do professionals capture, nurture, share and recycle their collective knowledge for the benefit of those they help? What if we could put in place altogether different ways of allowing people to access specialist knowledge? (p. 50). This combination of formal knowledge, know-how, expertise, experience and skills is "practical expertise" and in itself a form of the Commons (p. 53).

Externalisation on a "commons" basis comes about when the content is made available as a resource that is used, reused and shared at no cost with most if not all members of society. In the Commons of practical expertise, the motivation is to make this knowledge far more widely accessible. The professionals and others largely concede both ownership and control and the content is held in common for the benefit of all.

There are, however, problems with 'the Commons': Why would people cede ownership and control especially if it means foregoing income? Then there is Hardin's Tragedy of the Commons; might practical expertise be overused? There is a fear of underproduction as who covers the cost with the threat of piggy-backing (pp. 397–398). Remove the exclusivity and the incentive to produce diminishes. They question these arguments, however, as there are alternative motivations for operating in 'the Commons' an example being Wikipedia. Hardin's arguments don't appear to map easily onto the field of practical expertise (p. 402) as this increases in value as it is shared. Perhaps then the digital can be or become one of those thresholds into a different way of working in which this practical expertise is made more readily available to all.

In case one should become too idealistic about the digital, one should read Kate Crawford's *Atlas of AI* (2022) and her exposé of ways in which AI itself exploits the Commons of both natural resources such as lithium and human resources of labour as employed by Amazon (Chapters 1 and 2). She concludes "There are sustainable collective politics beyond value extraction: there are commons worth keeping, worlds beyond the market, and ways to live beyond discrimination and brutal modes of optimization. Our task is to chart a course there" (p. 227).

Another approach using the concept is that of the idea of the "Mental Commons", working on the understanding that out mental well-being is an essential component of a good and sustainable existence. This is against the background of increasing problems in this area both in the US and the UK. I borrow this from a colleague called Brendan Johnson who is a medic working in this field. He talks about human mental faculties, such as attention, memory, cognition, cultural and personal descriptive categories for understanding the world, the project of education. Inasmuch as human mental life bears the fingerprints of the past, culture and history are also part of the mental commons – inasmuch as humans are directed towards the future, our imagination and sense of hope are, too. The commons exist in reciprocal relationships with individual participants; thus, individuals contribute to the mental commons, but their mental lives are also formed by it. This relates back to the more radical ideas of Hardt and Negri and their proposal that the Commons is not just something that we encounter in a passive way, but something that still remains ahead to be created through new forms of subjectivity. Our relationships with others, therefore including the non-human of the natural world are essential to the Commons and may become a means of responding to the various crises we now face.

Finally, I wonder whether the concept could be expanded still further to talk about the Spiritual Commons. In other words, as well as our mental well-being there is also our spiritual well-being and ways in which that is both potentially damaged by the prevalence of the digital and of course our harmful relationships with the non-human generally, but also might discover those thresholds into deeper and healthier relationships. So much of what we experience are actually enclosures of the material and the spiritual and these need to be identified and resisted. Although I am not totally convinced as the concept is largely tied to the discipline of economics and therefore risks being too anthropocentric it does seem to contain the seeds of a more critical approach to both the ecological and the digital.

REFERENCES

Callicott, J. B. (2013). *Thinking like a planet: the land ethic and the earth ethic*. New York: Oxford University Press.

Crawford, K. (2022). *Atlas of AI: power, politics, and the planetary costs of artificial intelligence*. New Haven, CT: Yale University Press.

Hardt, M., & Negri, A. (2009). *Commonwealth*. Cambridge, MA: Belknap Press of Harvard University Press.
Leopold, A. (1970). *A Sand County almanac*. New York: Ballantine.
Northcott, M. S. (2014). *A political theology of climate change*. Society for Promoting Christian Knowledge SPCK.
Ostrom, E. (1992) Governing the Commons: The Evolution of Institutions for Collective Action. *Natural Resources Journal*, *32*, 415. Available at: https://digitalrepository.unm.edu/nrj/vol32/iss2/6
Raworth, K. (2022). *Doughnut economics: seven ways to think like a 21st-century economist*. London: Penguin Books.
Shrubsole, G. (2019). *Who owns England?* Glasgow: William Collins.
Susskind, R. E., & Susskind, D. (2022). *The future of the professions: how technology will transform the work of human experts*. Oxford: Oxford University Press.

8 On the Possibility of Artificial Sin

Sin, Sentience and Self

Paul Woods

INTRODUCTION

Rapid advances in artificial intelligence (AI) are prompting all kinds of discussions about the direction of its development and consequent effects on individuals and society. While much is being said about the ethics of AI involvement in a vast range of human endeavour, so far, Christian theology has not said much about the ethical or moral nature of AI systems themselves. This chapter considers the possibility and nature of sin associated with AIs by analogy with human sin and consideration of animal sentience. I begin with a brief introduction to AI, viewing the technology in terms of a continuum. Following this I explore the question of human distinctiveness vis-à-vis the animals. The issue of sentience is of central importance to the chapter and I therefore provide an extended treatment of the topic, again according to a continuum. Finally, I pull these strands together to derive an initial proposal for the idea of *artificial sin*. This is of significance for a volume which considers ethical aspects of the interaction between theology and the digital. Although the concept of artificial sin is developed by analogy with human sin initially as a theoretical exercise, the emergence of an AI with the capacity to sin, albeit in its own restricted way, would raise ethical issues of responsibility and accountability.

CONTEXT

Orthodox Christian theology looks at sin as a uniquely human problem. We are the only organism capable of sinful behaviour as a result of our unique status as God's image bearers who have gone against him. The original conception of AI, which for some remains its ultimate *telos*, was of computer systems which could completely replicate or mimic human intelligence (Negnevitsky, 2005, p. 7). While the state of the field of AI is contested, recent developments and press coverage suggest that computer systems are showing certain behaviours increasingly like our own. Against a background of and in creative contrast with orthodox Christian views of sin as a state of rebellion against a creator God, I posit the idea of 'artificial sin' as a consequence of AI. This does two things. First, the use of the term 'artificial' identifies this understanding of sin not as something which is not real and of no consequence,

DOI: 10.1201/9781003497950-11

although it does not have the element of rebellion against God's infinite holiness, but as a result and property of AI systems. Second, the kind of sin under discussion can exist between created entities only; there is no transcendent party, as there is in discussions of human sin.

ARTIFICIAL INTELLIGENCE

In his introduction to AI, Ertel uses a quotation from pioneer John McCarthy to summarise the original aim of the field as the development of 'machines that behave as though they were intelligent' (2017, p. 1). For engineers and computer scientists, the ultimate goal was to produce a machine 'showing intelligent behavior' (Ertel, 2017, p. 1). Such characteristics mesh with the Turing test, in which a person having a conversation with a computer would be unable to detect that he or she was talking to a machine rather than a human intelligence (Negnevitsky, 2005).

Reflecting the current, more modest state of affairs, Ertel describes the ability of computers to calculate and process data very quickly and the superiority of chess computers over many human players; he thus separates speed and accurate repeatability of calculations from adaptivity and learning (2017, p. 3). He explores *machine learning*, a subfield of AI, conceding that AI currently represents a wide range of specialised solutions for various tasks and there exists no single, general form of AI. This reflects the realisation in the 1970s that the best way to develop intelligent machines was to focus them on narrow tasks (Negnevitsky, 2005) because at that time it seemed beyond our ability to construct an artificially intelligent brain capable of learning and adapting to as wide a range of tasks as the human mind. Another important area within AI is *neural networks*, which allow computers to recognise photographs and handwriting, as well as speech from texts. These were significant improvements in the ability of AI systems, but their inherent limitation to narrow areas only served to reinforce the gulf between powerful expert systems and the human brain (Ertel, 2017, p. 9).

Summarising the current state of AI, Negnevitsky (2005) notes that rather than the general-purpose AI systems envisaged in the early 1950s, domain-specific expert systems use human knowledge and machine learning algorithms for problem solving. Under the title 'AI grows up' Ertel (2017) discusses expert systems, knowledge-based systems, data mining and information extraction; it is important to choose the right tool for the job. This reflects the categorisation of AI by Davenport et al. (2020, p. 27) into *narrow* (cannot be extended beyond a specific domain) and *general* (extendible to new domains). Although huge progress has been made, we are a long way from McCarthy's original dream in the mid-1950s.

Despite current technical realities, general AI, computer systems with general intelligence remain a 'holy grail' (Boden, 2016, p. 21). There is renewed interest in 'artificial general intelligence' or AGI (Boden, 2016, p. 22) as increased computer processing power and data storage and vastly improved algorithms hint at a time when programmed electronic machines might rival the human mind in all areas and abilities. In recent years, the term 'the Singularity' has become popular in AI circles. This is the moment when AI systems are judged to be as intelligent as people. At some point after the Singularity, AGI will give way to ASI, in which the S stands for 'Superhuman' (Boden, 2016, p. 147). AI optimists such as Kurzweil (2005) claim that AGI will be with us in less than a decade and that by the middle of this century ASI and other technologies will have dealt with all social and economic problems faced by humanity. Similar views have been expressed by AGI enthusiast Goertzel (Machine Learning Street Talk, 2021). However, according to Boden the three areas of 'language, creativity, and emotion' are very difficult for AI and if it cannot represent them then AGI is only an illusion (2016, p. 57).

This overview of the capabilities of AI suggests that it is helpful to think in terms of a continuum, from basic machine learning capabilities focused on specific, low-level tasks to the putative AGI at least as intelligent as a human being.

HUMAN DISTINCTIVENESS: SIN AND IMAGE

Having discussed the nature and types of AI, I now look briefly at human distinctiveness as it relates to the concepts of sin and the image of God as derived from the Bible, principally Genesis. Rather than provide a detailed treatment of the doctrine, the aim is to provide a baseline from which the notion of *artificial sin* might be developed analogically.

The Bible looks at sin almost exclusively in terms of human protagonists. In addition, most orthodox interpretations of the creation story of Genesis 1 and 2 assume an ontological separation between human beings and other living creatures. Such an anthropocentric position posits that only human beings are capable of sin, partly because our being created in the image of God has traditionally suggested some kind of ontological connection, as for example in Augustine's *De Trinitate*. However, recent scholarship (among which Walton, 2009; Bolos, 2018) has focused more on human beings as representative of God in a functional sense. In drawing some kind of analogy between human beings and AIs, for the purposes of this chapter there is no need to consider complex and speculative notions such as machines created in the image of human beings or having some kind of spirituality or transcendence.

A further important distinction between biblical notions of sin and the artificial sin associated with AI systems comes in terms of what I call its *directionality*. Biblical notions of sin include both a *vertical* and *horizontal* understanding. That is, the rebellion against the infinite creator in Genesis is seen as vertical, the finite, created being rejecting his sovereignty and authority. As the biblical narrative unfolds, the consequences of this vertical sin unfold in the horizontal plane, as Adam and Eve turn against each other and Cain murders Abel. Such a bidirectional distinction is also seen in the various commandments in both testaments and most clearly in the Decalogue; the first half of the Ten Commandments in the Hebrew Bible relate to the vertical aspect of human relationships, while the second half pertain more to the horizontal or created order. However, in exploring the possibility of sin existing in and committed by machines, there is no infinite or transcendent creator being. Although human beings are more complex than the computers they make, both are still finite, derivative entities. For this reason then, artificial sin operates only in the horizontal plane.

While traditional Christian anthropology separates human beings from animals by investing the idea of the divine image with ontological significance, a functional approach could allow us to view humankind and other living creatures as constituting a continuum. As the most intelligent creatures on the planet, human beings have the greatest ability and responsibility to represent the character and agenda of the creator. Other creatures with lower intelligence and simpler affective capabilities may still represent God, but in relatively restricted ways.

Such a functional approach meshes with recent research into the behaviour of the higher animals and the physical structure of their brains which questions the traditional human–animal dichotomy found in much Christian theology. The narrative of Genesis 1 and 2 can be taken as anthropocentric in that it is written to people rather than animals and does suggest that human beings are unique in being created ‘in the image of God’, yet we see a whole range of animal behaviours relating to cognitive ability, emotion, perception, social order and even altruism which forces us to see human beings and animals as forming a continuum rather than a simple binary.

ANIMAL SENTIENCE AS A PARADIGM

In thinking about the potential for AI systems to develop behaviours on the horizontal plane that could be described as artificial sin, it is useful to explore aspects of animal behaviour that might resemble those of AI systems. Expert systems and related technologies are extremely efficient at pattern matching and data analysis, although they are still far away from anything resembling the depth and breadth of human intelligence which is the goal of AGI (Boden, 2016, p. 22). While the still distant AGI technology would notionally include consciousness and self-awareness (if it indeed did parallel human intelligence), I wish to advance the idea of sentience as a potential measure of restricted, domain-specific and computationally simple machine intelligence. In other words, I explore the issue of whether current or soon-to-appear AI systems, still far from the level of AGI, could be considered as behaving in a similar way to sentient creatures.

DeGrazia (2020) explores the distinction between consciousness and sentience, claiming that consciousness means the ability to have subjective experience, but does not include the capacity for pleasant or unpleasant feelings. In other words, an entity which is conscious can be aware in some way of what is happening to it, but not have any notion of affect. Sentience involves the ability to have ‘quality of life or experiential welfare’; according to DeGrazia, ‘sentient beings have interests’ (2020, p. 17). A similar perspective is that of Ahmed and Corradi, whose general summary associates consciousness with cognition and sentience with affect (2022, p. 3). In their discussion of animal sentience, Browning and Birch adopt a broad definition of ‘the capacity for *any type of subjective experience*’ or ‘phenomenal consciousness’ (2022, p. 1). Note that the very same italicised phrase is understood by Barron and Klein (2016) as consciousness. Browning and Birch acknowledge that sentience is a contested concept and add the narrower understanding that sentience refers to the ability to assign positive or negative feelings to experiences, which they call *valence.* For them, valence applies to a range of experiences or sensations, such as pain and pleasure, anxiety and distress, and even hunger, thirst and warmth. Our apprehension of our experiences involves a combination of ‘sensory, affective and cognitive components’ (Browning & Birch, 2022, p. 1) and the affective factor associated with valence causes them to describe this narrower understanding as 'affective sentience'. This emphasis on feeling reminds them of Bentham's (1789, p. 309) comment on the intrinsic right to fair treatment of even 'the inferior animals'. In assessing what he calls the 'sensitivity of animals', an idea which seems to resemble the modern notion of 'sentience', Bentham argues that the most important factor is not whether a creature can talk or reason, but whether it can suffer.

According to DeGrazia (2020), there is evidence for sentience in mammals and birds, certain kinds of crustaceans and even insects; the idea of a continuum is useful here too. By contrast, Barron and Klein (2016) believe that insects are conscious but not sentient because they know what is happening to them and what they are doing, but are incapable of ascribing positive or negative feelings to their experiences. The trend in the scientific community to believe that sentience is present even in relatively simple organisms is significant. It means that an organism which does not have self-awareness can detect and respond to situations and events which it considers useful, pleasant, or harmful. It is worth noting that although most researchers follow the distinction between consciousness and sentience explored here, Lenharo describes sentience as 'an aspect of consciousness' (2024, p. 14). In passing, although there is now active research on plant sentience, I do not consider it here. First, the essential boundedness of current AIs in terms of hardware and software suggests parallels with the well-defined anatomical structure of animals, whereas plants have forms of rhizomatic connectivity much stronger than anything in the animal kingdom. Second, the ability of an animal organism to respond to a stimulus with an independent action of some kind invites comparison with a standalone computer system.

Scholars approach the issue of sentience from a number of angles. For some, response to pain is a marker of sentience, while for others, the capacity for affect is of greater significance. In addition, organisational behaviour among lower creatures and animal cognitive structures also appear in research on sentience. DeGrazia's (2020) basic principle is that 'sentient beings are capable of having pleasant or unpleasant experiences' and his study focuses on pain, as it is relatively easy to assess among creatures which do not express themselves in language. He notes that there are various means of identifying the presence of pain, including neurochemical receptors, responses from a central nervous system (of one form or another), and protecting of injured body parts by the creature. He also adds natural and man-made analgesic pain relief and resultant changed behaviour, learned avoidance and what he calls 'trade-offs'. Consider a rat which is able to weigh up different factors and decide whether to endure some degree of suffering in order to obtain food or water.

DeGrazia (2020) focuses on pain in his examination of sentience in different animal classes. He begins by describing the physical structures of animal brains. His comparison of pain in mammals and birds reveals that the avian dorsal ventricular ridge functions in a similar way to the mammalian cerebral cortex. Browning and Birch (2022) note the physical similarity between the 'central complex' of the insect brain and the mid-brain of vertebrates; for them this may suggest a common ability for subjective experience. The acceptance of a central complex refutes earlier theories that suggested a defuse system of ganglia throughout an insect's body. Barron and Klein (2016) introduce us to the jewel wasp, which injects cockroaches with a special kind of venom. The venom acts on the cockroach's brain to remove all volitional ability, producing a passive state in which the victim is led by the wasp into its burrow. The unfortunate cockroach is still able to understand its environment and control its legs as it walks helplessly to its death, its zombification suggesting a separation between simple cognitive processing and the exercise of will. It appears that creatures with fundamentally different brain structures may share basic sentience.

Turning to the experience of pain, there is considerable evidence for sentience in reptiles, which feel pain, show stress when handled, and exhibit aversion to unpleasant tastes. Apparently, amphibians do not exhibit 'trade-off behaviour', protect injured body parts or show learned avoidance, suggesting a lower level of sentience. There is thus less evidence for sentience in cold-blooded creatures than in higher animals (DeGrazia, 2020).

Finally come the arthropods. Bees apparently do not have pain receptors but do respond to unpleasant stimuli. It is unclear whether they exhibit protective behaviour and learned avoidance (DeGrazia, 2020). Several scholars believe that bees and other insects are conscious but not sentient; they know what is happening to them and their environment but do not appear to have feelings about it. For Browning and Birch, the continued feeding and mating of injured insects do not fulfil DeGrazia's (2020) specification of sentience, yet they also quote research suggesting that bees demonstrate optimism after being given 'an expected sugar reward' (2022, p. 4).

Other authors have used affect to examine sentience in animals. Kujala (2017) looks at domestic dogs, concluding that they have lower self-awareness than human beings, because they do not pass the Gallup mirror self-recognition test. However, they spend more time inspecting the urine markings of other dogs than they do their own and exhibit a clear *self-other* distinction (2017, p. 9), complex social behaviours demonstrating sentience. Dogs also display inequity aversion; if one dog is rewarded for carrying out a task and another is not, the deprived animal shows clear reluctance or refusal to carry out the task next time (Kujala, 2017, p. 10). They also engage in conflict mediation, a third party attempting to come between two opposing parties, and demonstrate postconflict reconciliation. Finally, dogs manifest altruistic behaviour, such as pulling a rope to feed another dog, but only if the recipient animal is known to them (Kujala, 2017, p. 13).

Marino and Merskin (2019) describe sheep sentience in some depth. Sheep recognise faces and exhibit preference for conspecifics. Their ability to recognise different facial expressions helps them negotiate social group hierarchies. Sheep possess emotional valence and intensity, demonstrating different degrees of positive and negative emotions, particularly through 'ear posture' (Marino & Merskin, 2019, p. 8). They are well known for their ability to feel and demonstrate fear, certain familiar sequences of activities producing fear and stress before an event happens. Lambs respond negatively when the reward for completing a task is less than previous experience has led them to expect and sheep react negatively when they feel let down (Marino & Merskin, 2019, p. 10). Due to their 'social buffering', when an individual sheep is faced with a situation causing stress or fear, the presence of conspecifics reduces the negative response (Marino & Merskin, 2019, p. 11). When sheep are socially isolated, pictures of other familiar sheep reduce stress, but those of goats do not. Finally, sheep have distinct personalities, with a particular distinction between leaders and followers.

The more cognitive aspects of sentience are addressed by DeGrazia (2020) in his comments on the 'remarkable capacity to learn' of cephalopods, octopuses, squid and cuttlefish. They can pull levers to obtain food, open jars and squirt water to turn off lights. They also engage in trade-offs in order to obtain food. DeGrazia (2020) assesses cephalopods as having the same level of sentience as reptiles. In addition, male cuttlefish have been observed changing the colours on different sides of their bodies to deceive male and female conspecifics (Brown, Garwood & Williamson, 2012).

Another interesting research area in animal sentience is the organisational and cooperative behaviour of arthropods, 'agents whose goals – and therefore interest – can be frustrated' (Delon et al., 2020, p.2). Similar to human beings, arthropod decision-making is carried out by reference to systems beyond their immediate awareness. Delon et al. detail the ability of bees to choose among various options in order to realise a particular aim (2020, p. 2). It is known that ants remember stimuli that have caused them harm in the past and take evasive action. It appears that arthropods can assess positive and negative aspects of their physical states within a given environment and make appropriate responses. The choice of a course of action is influenced by factors beyond the physical data of a given context and reflects subliminal processes and mental structures beyond the purely cognitive. A number of researchers have thus stretched their definition of sentience. Discussing what is admittedly controversial and contested material, Browning and Birch (2022) recognise sentience in bees, because of their 'complex behaviour and cognitive abilities'. DeGrazia (2020) agrees; bees do not feel pain but are known for their ability to cooperate for a shared purpose.

Similar to bees, spiders manifest a wide range of learning styles and an elementary understanding of numbers (Japyassu & Laland, 2017). Jumping spiders plan their routes and temporarily lose sight of their prey in order to ambush their victims at a moment of their choice (Japyassu & Laland, 2017, p. 378). They can also change their diet according to their circumstances. Some spiders even change the way they walk when visiting the web of a different species of spider in order to deceive the owner. They know how their movements might be interpreted by a predator and adjust them accordingly.

Finally, it is necessary to look briefly at different modes of interacting with the outside world. Certain lower creatures possess lower degrees of sentience than mammals, yet interact with their environments in more specialised ways. In the higher animals the central nervous system within the organism is co-locational with the primary conceptual apparatus. Such creatures perceive their environments through sensory organs which are part of them and directly connected to the brain (Japyassu & Laland, 2017), allowing them to deal with complex environments and situations.

By contrast, web-dwelling spiders use the threads of their webs as a form of 'extended conception' (Japyassu & Laland, 2017, p. 375). The sensitivity of the web to the presence and movements of an intruder or potential victim functions as a form of sense organ outside the body of the spider. While the central cognition of the higher animals allows them to model the external world inside the brain, the extended cognition of spiders means that representation inside the brain is less important (Japyassu & Laland, 2017). They can interpret precisely the vibrations of their webs and discern what kind of organism is entering their broader conceptual world. The spider's reliance on its web, a fixed external structure, means it has to deal with a narrower range of data types and within these constraints is remarkably successful in achieving its aims. A different arrangement again is the 'neural modeling of space' (Barron & Klein, 2016, p. 4904) which happens in the brain of a flying insect as it moves at high speed, often evading physical objects and predators. Here there is no possibility of extended conceptual apparatus beyond the body. The flying insect processes a vast amount of data relating to speed, distance, height and threats, yet of course may repeatedly bump into a window, more evidence of a highly specialised and narrow form of conceptual processing. These two different cases show that creatures of lower sentience are very successful even though, or because, they interact with the world very differently from the higher animals.

We may thus consider a spider or a bee as a highly specialised expert system. As complex an animal as a dog has lower sentience than a human being; it may not have the range of affective capability that we have, yet the canine sense of smell seems to show remarkable similarity to the pattern matching of AI systems. I have included this amount of detail in order to demonstrate not only that sentience is a continuum, but also that it manifests in different aspects of animal behaviour and different degrees of specialisation.

ARTIFICIAL SIN

To explore the possibility of artificial sin, I propose that an AI system can be thought of as similar to a sentient creature. It has been shown that AI forms a continuum from narrow, expert systems and machine learning technologies to a putative AGI. The current state of AI is located at the lower end of that continuum, although the discipline is developing very quickly.

It seems credible that AIs at or just beyond the current state of development could soon possess or develop a form of sentience equivalent to that of a lower animal such as a bee or spider. This kind of AI system would be able to understand its environment in terms of a narrow range of data inputs such as those used by a spider. Expert systems focused on narrow tasks and datasets could be considered as employing something analogous to the extended conception of a spider in its web.

Given that sentience concerns the ability of an organism to assess its circumstances and respond affectively, showing preference or aversion and taking appropriate action, a relatively simple AI could behave in a similar fashion. For this reason, if their evolving algorithms were flexible enough, they could make positive or negative assessments of particular input data or the conclusions they have drawn. AIs which examine cardiology scans for heart defects have an innate, designed ability to recognise data representing something negative or unpleasant, and are thus able to differentiate between 'good and bad' according to the algorithms within, even though they are not conscious as we are, as we have seen above.

AI systems are trained on vast datasets and can then detect patterns or even produce something novel. Consider the work of Gatys, Ecker and Bethge (2016), in which neural networks were able to separate the *content* and *style* of classic paintings such as Munch's *The Scream*. The style of the painting was then applied to a photograph of a street of houses in Tuebingen to produce an *image* which expressed the primary features of the houses but through the fluid and chaotic style of the famous disturbing painting. A less successful creation by Botnik Studios (n.d.) saw an AI system given all of the Harry Potter novels and then produce a substandard story described as 'equally insane and hilarious' in which Ron Weasley eats Hermione Granger's family. These two examples of AI creativity correspond to the responses to external stimuli by a sentient entity. It is surely not much beyond the capabilities of current technology for an AI to identify *The Scream* as negative in one way or another or conclude that Harry Potter characters should not eat each other, thus making an affective judgement. In the same vein, the current problem of deepfake pornographic images could produce a similar reaction. If an AI were given suitable input data and the ability to learn and amend its algorithms, it could decide that deepfake porn is wrong, particularly if the images it were processing clearly depicted underage participants or incidents of coercion. By the same token, different input data and algorithms might incline an AI towards the unpleasant or criminal.

Discussions of sentience mention the ability of an organism to make affective decisions or assessments about their own situation, such as sensing pain and evaluating taste, for example. However, sentience also involves evaluation of the presence of Others (as opposed to the Self) and the possibility of threats. Bees cooperate for a common purpose and spiders are sensitive to the presence of Others in their webs, whether as intruders or potential food. Sentience thus requires some sense of the Self-Other distinction and acknowledgement of the presence of the Other, directly or through its influence. Here, I am reminded of the psychology of Lacan, in particular his 'mirror stage' (1977, p. 2) in the early development of the human person. It is during this stage, which lasts from the age of 6–18 months, that a child becomes aware of its own Self and the Other (Sarup, 1993, p. 22), who is almost always the child's mother, and begins to understand the separation of itself from her. It is clear that even a small child is able to assess its situation and environment and react accordingly – a child who is just able to walk is thus sentient. The implication of the separation from its mother and the emergence of sentience is that an entity which may or may not have attained consciousness is able to evaluate its circumstances, albeit in a rudimentary fashion, from a self-focused perspective. In that sense, then, inasmuch as simple organisms and by implication narrow AIs can take account of their needs, opportunities and threats, they are capable and indeed destined to sin in the horizontal sense. If we take the horizontal, interpersonal understanding of sin, neglecting for this paper vertical sin against a transcendent creator, then any entity which recognises its own existence separate from Others immediately around it and prioritises itself has no alternative but to sin.

The final issue to address is whether artificial sin is a matter of intention or action. In other words, could what might correspond to a mental state potentially leading to but not yet resulting in action be considered artificially sinful? If a sentient machine could assess a particular situation as threatening to itself or the interests of a person or other AI associated with it, such that it sensed a need to protect its own interests against those of an external Other, would such a sentient *state* be understood as sinful? Or is it safer to assume that an AI system would only be identified as (artificially) sinful if it took *action*? Unless we were to monitor the data and performance of the algorithms within the AI, we would have no way of understanding the system before it took action of some kind. With regard to human sin, orthodox Christian theology is clear that both state of mind and course of action are equally capable of manifesting sin. Concerning sinful action by machines, by learning from vast datasets, an AI might not only detect something 'wrong' or 'right', as defined by its database, but perhaps alter its output data and produce conclusions other than those expected from the input data and the algorithms installed. The AI's assessment of a given situation as represented by a real-time dataset might then move it to action. Computer systems are increasingly interconnected and automated; financial data, user profiles, weather data, etc., could be altered or even falsified in accordance with the machine's sentient response or motivation. Where AIs have the ability to control physical systems by means of digital-mechanical interfaces, security doors could be locked or unlocked, sluices of dams opened or closed, and road or rail signals configured safely or dangerously. This kind of behaviour seems increasingly plausible and raises questions not only about the origin and nature of artificial sin, but also about responsibility and accountability. An AI which sins artificially would suffer no ultimate judgement at the hands of a transcendent creator, but who would be responsible for a machine which blocked access to funds for a group of people whom it accessed as unsuitable or suspicious, opened a dam, or intentionally caused a mid-air collision? Does artificial sin imply artificial responsibility, in which the machine only is held accountable for its actions, especially unexpected ones occurring due to the behaviour of the algorithms within? One wonders about the role and position of system designers and programmers. We might draw parallels with a pet dog which has recently bitten someone in a park. In law, the owner is responsible, but for a sentient creature which as far as we know has no sense of a transcendent creator, where does accountability really lie? The point is that artificial sin as conceived of in this chapter is only artificial in the sense that it can be produced by an AI; the emergence and demonstration of a sinful nature in a machine could be as real as for a human being.

CONCLUSION

Sentience is an attribute of to higher and lower animals, which enables them to make affective judgements in sometimes fairly narrow domains. It is reasonable to equate the level of sentience of AI systems with that of fairly simple creatures, in that both can determine whether situations they face or deal with are positive or negative. An entity which can identify itself in the presence of another, especially with regard to the possibility of threats or advantages, can make decisions which favour itself and potentially disadvantage the Other in a Self-Other dyad. Such a focus on the interest of the Self, potentially at the expense of the Other, fulfils some of the traditional Christian understanding of sin between created beings. In that sense, it can be postulated that before very long, narrow AIs and expert systems may have the capacity to sin, in intent or action, in ways analogous to human beings. For this reason, I claim that 'artificial sin' could soon exist, working in the horizontal, finite plane but absent with regard to a transcendent creator.

REFERENCES

Ahmed, A., & Corradi, C., (2022). *Animal Sentience and Consciousness: A Review of Current Research*. London: Nuffield Council on Bioethics.

Barron, A.B., & Klein, C. (2016). What insects can tell us about the origins of consciousness. *Proceedings of the National Academy of Sciences of the United States of America*, 113(18), 4900–4908.

Bentham, J. (1789). *An introduction to the principles of morals and legislation*. London: T. Payne and Son.

Boden, M. (2016). *Artificial intelligence: A very short introduction*. Oxford: Oxford University Press.

Bolos, A. (2018). A functionalist account of human uniqueness. *Faith and Philosophy*, 35(3), 326–344. Doi:10.5840/faithphil2018614106

Botnik Studios. (n.d.). *Harry Potter*. https://botnik.org/content/harry-potter.html

Brown, C., Garwood, M., & Williamson, J. (2012). It pays to cheat: Tactical deception in a cephalopod social signalling system. *Biology Letters*, 8(5), 729–32. Doi:10.1098/rsbl.2012.0435

Browning, H., & Birch, J. (2022). Animal sentience. *Philosophy Compass*, 17(5), 1–14. Doi:10.1111/phc3.12822

Davenport, T., Guha, A., Grewal, D., & Bressgott, T. (2020). How artificial intelligence will change the future of marketing. *Journal of the Academy of Marketing Science*, 48, 24–42. Doi:10.1007/s11747-019-00696-0

DeGrazia, D. (2020). Sentience and consciousness as bases for attributing interest and moral status: Considering the evidence and speculating slightly beyond. In L. Johnson, A. Fenton, & A. Shriver (Eds.), *Neuro ethics and nonhuman animals* (pp.17–31). Berlin: Springer.

Delon, N., Cook, P., Bauer, G., & Harley, H. (2020). Consider the agent in the arthropod. *Animal Sentience*, 5(29), 1–5.

Ertel, W. (2017). *Introduction to artificial intelligence*. Cham: Springer International Publishing.

Gatys, L., Ecker, A., & Bethge, M. (2016). Image style transfer using convolutional neural networks. *Proceedings of 2016 IEEE Conference on Computer Vision and Pattern Recognition (CVPR), Las Vegas*, pp. 2414–2423.

Japyassu, H., & Laland, K. (2017). Extended spider cognition. *Animal Cognition*, 20(3), 375–95. Doi:10.1007/s10071-017-1069-7

Kujala, M.V. (2017) Canine emotions as seen through human social cognition. *Animal Sentience* 14(1), 2–34. Doi:10.51291/2377-7478.1114

Kurzweil, R. (2005). *The Singularity is near: When humans transcend biology*. London: Penguin.

Lacan, J. (1977). *Écrits: A selection* (A. Sheridan, Trans.). London: Routledge.

Lenharo, M. (2024). Are bees sentient? Animal consciousness needs a rethink. *Nature*, 629, 14–15.

Machine Learning Street Talk. (2021, August 11). #58Artificial general intelligence. Dr Ben Goerztel [Video]. Youtube. Retrieved from https://www.youtube.com/watch?v=sw8IE3MX1SY

Marino, L., & Merskin, D. (2019). Intelligence, complexity, and individuality in sheep. *Animal Sentience*, 25(1), 1–25. Doi:10.51291/2377-7478.1374

Negnevitsky, M. (2005). *Artificial intelligence: A guide to intelligent systems*. Harlow: Pearson Education Limited.

Sarup, M. (1993). *An introductory guide to post-structuralism and postmodernism*. Athens, GA: University of Georgia Press.

Walton, J. (2009). *The lost world of Genesis One: Ancient cosmology and the origins debate*. Lisle, IL: IVP Academic.

9 Neural Networks and Postdigital Ethics

Peter Haslehurst and Andrew Bevan

INTRODUCTION

This chapter had its origins in a series of conversations between Dr. Peter Haslehurst and Rev. Andrew Bevan in 2019 and 2020. We offer a brief introduction to the workings of artificial neural networks (ANNs), which underpin many of the most strikingly powerful artificial intelligences (AI), while drawing attention to their deep roots in neuroscience. We will explore the relationship between the human brain and these systems, highlight some implications for postdigital ethics, and offer some thoughts about how the sources referenced might suggest ways in which God interacts with humans, and technology, drawing on the science in this chapter.

CONTEXT

The postdigital recognises a radical change in the human condition rather than an event or epoch (Jandrić et al., 2018). Writing about 'brain-like' ANNs Bostrom noted the requirement of sufficiently powerful processors for them to become practically useful (Bostrom, 2014, p. 10). He also reported that there were 150,000 academic papers (in 2014) concerned with their development. Subsequently, with greatly increased power, the ready availability of economically viable computer chips has brought what was previously the subject of science fiction into the latest mobile phones and laptops, new vehicles and myriad other day-to-day applications. *The Magnificent Seven* is how the biggest US tech companies (Nvidia, Meta, Amazon, Alphabet, Apple, Microsoft, Tesla) have become known to investors (Rennison, 2024). Their range of activities and the scale of resources deployed indicate the current importance of and hopes for AI. This could be viewed as a product of human ingenuity: a combination of research, entrepreneurial acumen, commitments to support and apply academic research, human collaboration and cooperation, courageous use of enormous quantities of risk capital: An extensive postdigital ethical challenge and not much to do with God, then?

John Reader was keen to include our chapter so we feel constrained by his untimely absence. We expected his help to reflect on some of its implications for theology and ethics since we do not feel competent to add to the extensive philosophical analysis undertaken by him and others. As John remained a working parish minister to the end of his life so it is without apology that we contribute as two practitioners who are also practicing Christians.

DOI: 10.1201/9781003497950-12

SYNAPTIC TRANSMISSION IN ANIMAL BRAINS

Working in a cellular neuroscience laboratory, Peter explored the functioning of the highly specialised brain cells known as *neurons*, about 85 billion of which (plus at least as many support cells) make up the average human brain. Figure 9.1 shows a typical neuron which, while still alive and functioning normally, was filled with a fluorescent dye. The cell body (or *soma*) is clearly visible, about 30 microns in length (i.e., 30 thousandths of a millimetre), surrounded by an extensive arbour of *dendrites*, tree-like structures which grow out of the soma.

The lower half of Figure 9.1 zooms in on one particular dendrite, where numerous tiny outgrowths (known as *spines*) can clearly be seen protruding from the dendrite. Spines are typically anything from 0.2 to 1 micron in diameter. These images were acquired using light with a wavelength of about 0.5 microns – quite close to the theoretical limits of what it is possible to resolve with a light microscope. Spines are critically important for brain function because of what they represent: each spine is the postsynaptic half of a *synapse*, the connection between two neurons across which information flows.

The dendritic arbour can be thought of as the neuron's input structure. Every spine, of which there might be as many as 100,000 (in the case of a human neuron), receives signals from a different presynaptic neuron. The corresponding output structure is called the *axon*, a thin, threadlike structure which emerges from the soma then branches and projects over quite long distances (millimetres or even centimetres!), making synapses with a large number of postsynaptic neurons. The axon typically has hundreds or even thousands of *boutons*, microscopic swellings, each of which represents the presynaptic half of a synapse. Figure 9.2 shows an image of a neuron where the axon is clearly visible. The lower half of Figure 9.2 zooms in on a small portion of the axon where a few presynaptic boutons are visible as bright swellings.

Using an electron microscope to image a single bouton reveals dozens of little spheres. These *vesicles* each contain a few thousand of molecules of *neurotransmitter* (see Figure 9.3). The brain makes use of several different kinds of neurotransmitter such as acetyl choline, serotonin, GABA, or dopamine, but in humans by far the most common is *glutamate*. Release of neurotransmitter is driven by the arrival of an electrical spike (the *action potential*) travelling down the axon to the presynaptic bouton. This spike consists of a very rapid change in the axon's *membrane potential*. At rest the inside of the axon sits at minus 70 millivolts relative to the outside. When the spike arrives this rapidly changes, peaking at around plus 40 millivolts compared to the outside, and just as rapidly bouncing back to its resting potential of minus 70 millivolts. The whole process can be over in as short a time as 2 milliseconds. Each travelling electrical spike originates at the presynaptic neuron and travels along the axon to the bouton, where it causes (by means of some elaborate cellular machinery) one or more vesicles to merge with the cell membrane, spilling their contents into the *synaptic cleft* (the gap between the presynaptic and postsynaptic membranes, with a width of about 20 nanometers, that is, 20 millionths of a millimetre) (Kandel et al., 2021, Chapters 7 & 8).

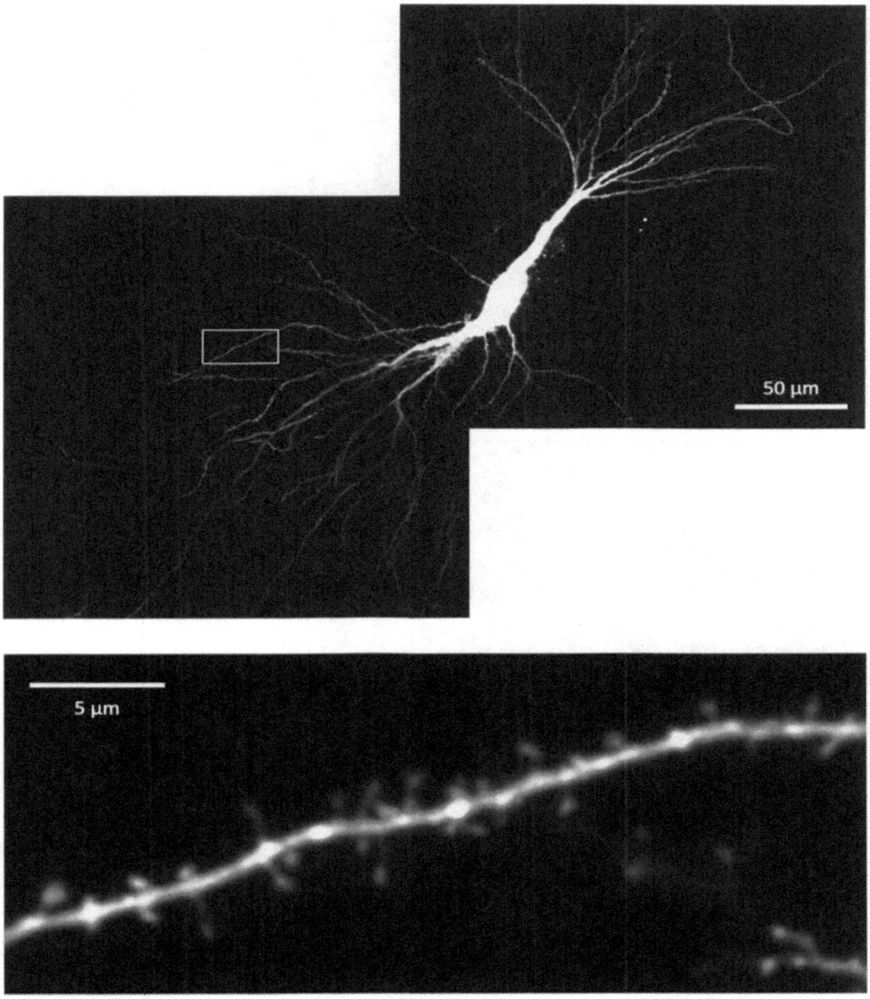

FIGURE 9.1 Confocal microscope image of a living neuron filled with fluorescent dye. The neuron was in a brain slice taken from the hippocampus of a rat pup. The hippocampus is a brain structure concerned with memory and navigation through space. The zoomed-in detail shows a section of dendrite and the spines which cover it. Notice the spines are highly diverse in size and shape. Images acquired by Peter Haslehurst at the Nigel Emptage Group, Department of Pharmacology, University of Oxford.

The postsynaptic membrane has many *receptors* embedded in it – specialised proteins which can detect the presence of neurotransmitter such as glutamate in the synaptic cleft. Each receptor also functions as a channel which can open to allow the passage of ions (such as sodium) across the cell membrane into the spine. When glutamate is detected these channels open and positive ions flow into the spine,

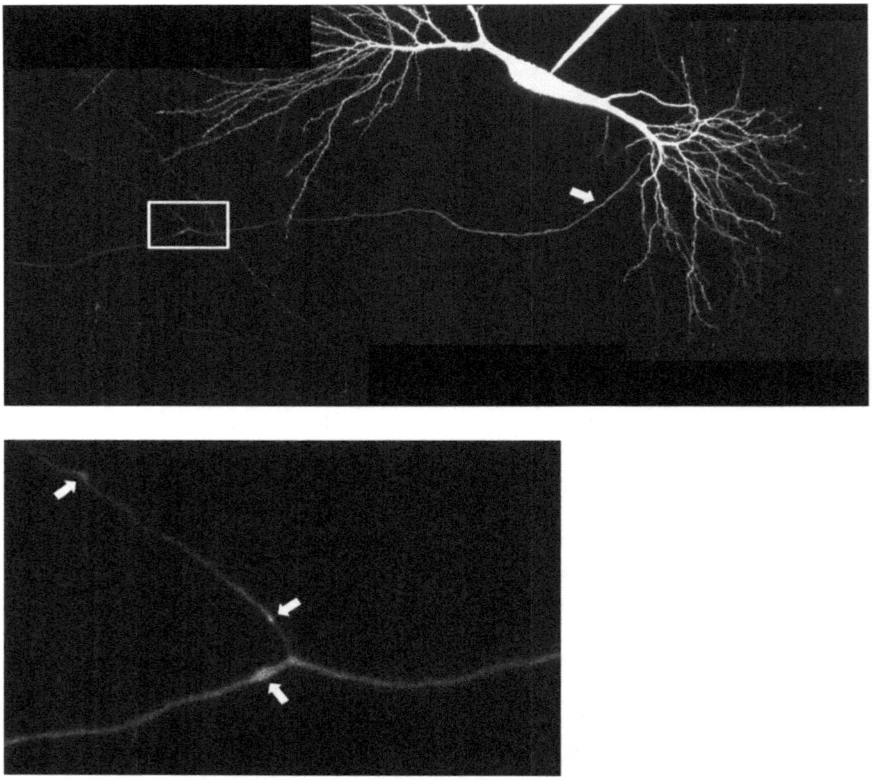

FIGURE 9.2 Another hippocampal neuron. The axon is very apparent in the top panel, emerging from the base of a dendrite (arrow), and is smooth and slender, very different to the dendrites. (Also visible at the top of the image is the glass pipette I used to fill the cell with dye.) The zoomed-in detail (bottom panel) shows an axon branch point. Notice the bright swellings (arrows) – these are presynaptic boutons. Images acquired by Peter Haslehurst at the Nigel Emptage Group, Department of Pharmacology, University of Oxford.

producing a small electrical blip in the postsynaptic cell, known as the excitatory postsynaptic potential (EPSP). Recall that the postsynaptic cell possesses as many as 100,000 spines, and that each spine is experiencing the occasional or frequent arrival of EPSP's. These propagate down the dendritic arbour into the soma where they summate. If at some point these summed EPSP's reach a certain threshold the soma will produce an action potential of its own, which in turn propagates down the axon to its many presynaptic boutons, where the process of synaptic transmission begins again (Kandel et al., 2021, Chapters 7 & 8). Intriguingly, the action potential is an all or nothing phenomenon: it either happens or it doesn't, but if it does happen it has a stereotyped amplitude. Information is conveyed by the number and frequency of the spikes, but not their size. This is reminiscent of a digital signal, but when the spike reaches a synapse it produces a little cloud of neurotransmitter – very definitely an analog signal. Then in the soma these incoming analog

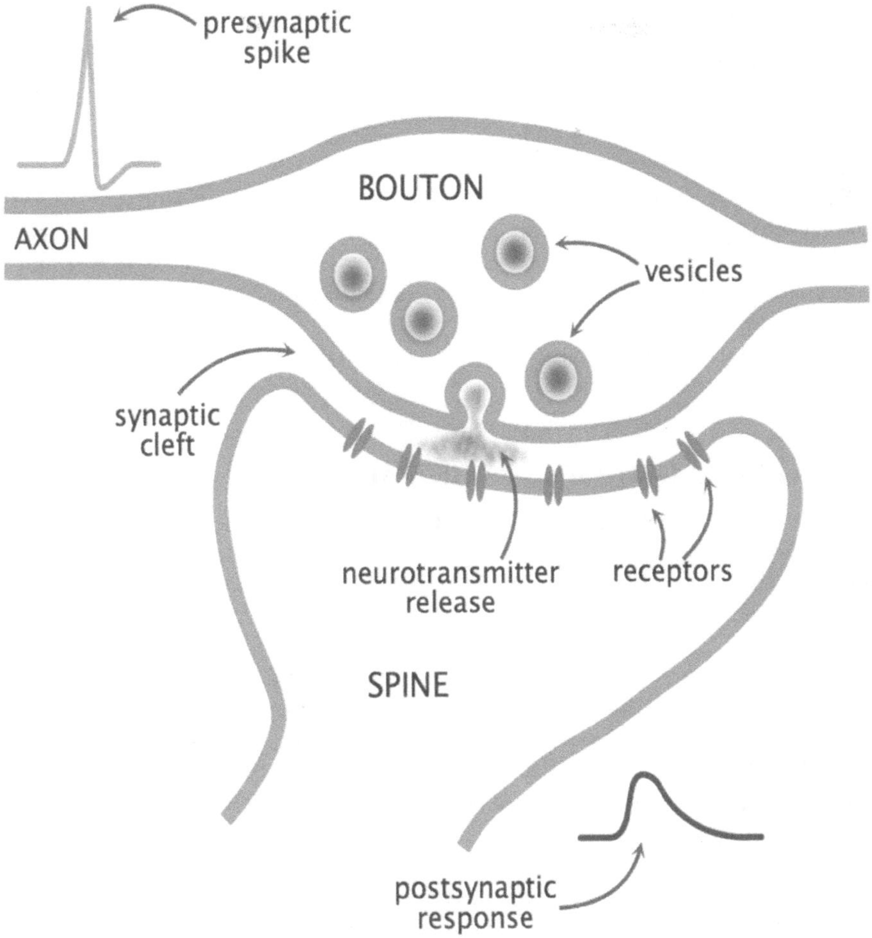

FIGURE 9.3 Sketch diagram of a synapse, showing the pre- and postsynaptic sides of the structure (bouton and spine, respectively). The bouton has a population of membrane-delimited spheres (vesicles), each containing a standard amount of neurotransmitter (such as glutamate). When a spike (action potential) arrives along the axon one or more vesicles fuse with the bouton's membrane to release neurotransmitter into the synaptic cleft. This process (whether or not a vesicle fuses) is probabilistic. The postsynaptic membrane is studded with receptors which convert the chemical signal back into an electrical one. Diagram by Peter Haslehurst.

signals are integrated to produce spikes in its own axon – back to a digital signal again.

PROBABILISTIC TRANSMISSION

The account of synaptic transmission outlined above is misleading in one important regard: the arrival of the action potential at the presynaptic bouton does *not* reliably result in the release of neurotransmitter into the synaptic cleft. In fact this process is probabilistic; for every 10 spikes that arrive at the bouton, only 2 or 3 of them (chosen seemingly at random) will actually produce a cloud of neurotransmitter. In other words, a typical synapse has a *release probability* of about 0.2–0.3 (Branco & Staras, 2009). This seems bizarre – of all the (presumably useful) information arriving at the synapse, 70–80% of it is simply discarded.

A modern computer (e.g., a laptop or a phone) functions by executing *algorithms* – a sequence of steps which given the same input data will always produce the same output. The probabilistic nature of synaptic transmission strongly suggests that the brain is not a computer, and that a human's cognitive functions, such as sensation, attention, learning, memory, language, decision making, motor function, etc., cannot be understood as the execution of algorithms (no matter how complex). This insight is clearly relevant to our discussion of ethics in the postdigital context.

SYNAPTIC PLASTICITY AND ARTIFICIAL NEURAL NETWORKS

Another layer of understanding that must be added to our discussion of synaptic transmission is that our memories are encoded in the strengths of a population of synapses. Each synapse can be thought of as having a transmission strength – the arrival of an action potential at a weak synapse produces a very small EPSP, whereas a strong synapse produces a much larger EPSP. When a new skill is being learned or a new memory acquired, a large number of synapses on a large number of neurons are all changing their strengths to encode those memories or skills. Moreover, this seems to be a physical phenomenon – the spines actually grow or shrink physically. This ability of synapses to alter their transmission strength (and of the corresponding spines to change in size and shape) is known as *plasticity* and is a critically important property of synapses (Matsuzaki et al., 2004).

We turn now to ANNs, which are a key component of many of the AI systems that are currently stirring public debate, such as ChatGPT, AlphaGo, AlphaFold, etc. ANNs were originally inspired by a few very basic facts about the way neurons work (McLeod et al., 1998):

1. **Neurons integrate incoming information**: moment by moment each neuron is receiving incoming signals from thousands or tens of thousands of other neurons. At each of these synapses, whenever an action potential arrives it produces a small electrical signal (EPSP) in the postsynaptic cell. In the neuron's soma these signals are integrated and a 'decision' is made whether or not to output an action potential along its own axon.
2. **Each synapse has a transmission strength**: incoming signals (action potentials) arrive frequently at each of a neuron's synapses. The size of an action potential does not change, but the electrical response (EPSP) seen in the postsynaptic cell varies from synapse to synapse. Some connections are strong – when an action potential arrives it produces a larger response. Other synapses are weaker – they produce a smaller postsynaptic response.

3. **Neurons are organised in layers**: for example, in the retina there is a layer of light-detecting neurons, then a second layer of neurons, and then a third layer which connects with another layer of neurons in the thalamus (a pair of egg-shaped bodies at the base of the cortex). From the thalamus visual information is passed to the visual cortex which again is organised in layers: primary visual cortex, then secondary visual cortex, tertiary visual cortex, etc.
4. **Synapses are plastic**: the strength of a synapse can change over time, often driven by experiences such as acquiring memories or learning skills. It is believed that a memory of a particular episode, for example, consists of the pattern of the strengths of a large number of connections between a particular population of neurons.

In neural networks we take these four principles and make an artificial version (see Figure 9.4). The computer simulates a simple artificial neuron which has many input connections, each of which has a strength (or weight). The artificial neuron also has an output signal – which is passed to every neuron in the next layer.

The computer keeps track of all the input signals as a list of numbers, for example: 0.6, 0.2, 0.4, etc. It keeps track of the input connection weights as another list of

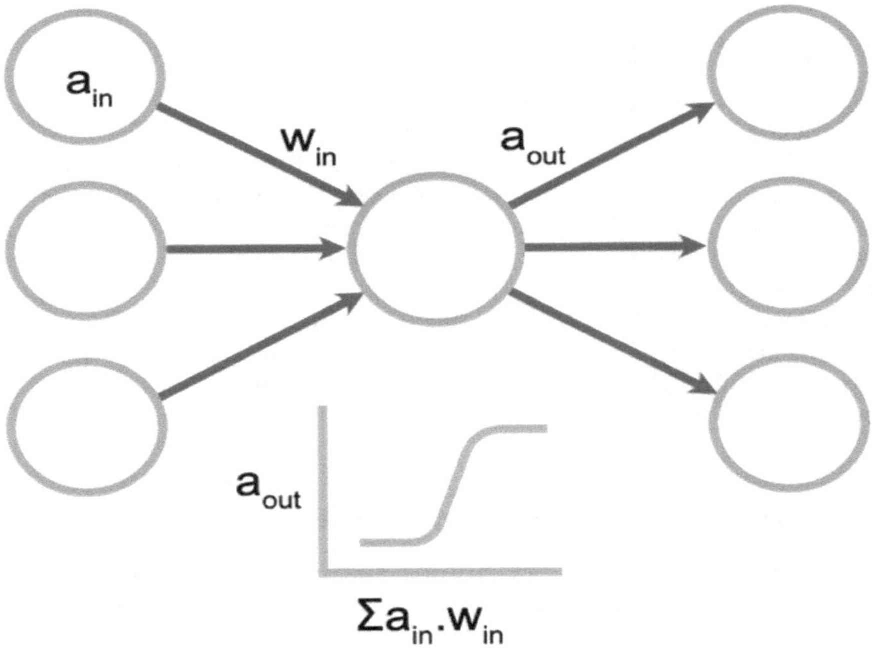

FIGURE 9.4 Sketch diagram of a single unit ('neuron') in an artificial neural network. Each input neuron has an activity ain, and is connected to the unit by a connection of weight win. The unit sums or integrates the weighted input activities, and uses a sigma (or other) function to calculate the output activity aout, which is propagated to every unit in the next layer. Diagram by Peter Haslehurst, adapted from McLeod et al. (1998).

numbers, for example: 0.1 (very weak), 0.9 (very strong), etc. All the inputs to the neuron are integrated in some way – in the simplest case this would just be a question of multiplying each input by its weight and averaging the results. Then the neuron's output is calculated using one of many possible functions, for example, a sigmoid function (see Figure 9.4).

There are two schools of neural network researchers: those who are working to create an ANN as close as possible to how the biological brain works, and those who want to make something effective and efficient, whether or not it is biologically relevant. This choice between biological plausibility and computational efficiency, will influence the choices made when designing artificial neurons.

Now that we have grasped how one artificial neuron works we can start to string them together in layers. In a very simple ANN known as a *pattern associator,* there is an input layer of neurons in which each neuron receives a single user-defined input (see Figure 9.5) (McLeod et al., 1998). The user defines a pattern of activity on the input layer: for example it might be a binary code representing a letter, or it might be a number between 0 and 1024 giving the brightness of a pixel in an image – there are many possibilities. Next there is a second layer of neurons which takes inputs from every neuron in the input layer. Each of these connections from the input layer has a weight.

TRAINING THE NETWORK

Consider an ANN where the input neurons are set with a binary code representing a letter, let us say 'A', and the output neurons are set to another binary code representing the letter you want to associate 'A' with, let us say 'B' (see Figure 9.5). We might also want to train the network to associate [input] 'C' with [output] 'D', [input] 'E' with [output] 'F', etc. (This kind of association is one of the key things that human memory does.) So we present the neural network with these pairs in training sessions: A → B, C → D, E → F, a few dozen times.

Every time a pair is presented a rule (specified by the ANN's designer) is invoked to modify the weights of every connection (recall our discussion about synaptic plasticity above). After training, if the network is presented with an 'A' on the input layer, it will produce a 'B' on the output layer; if presented with a 'C' it will produce a 'D', etc.

PROPERTIES OF ARTIFICIAL NEURAL NETWORKS

Even a simple ANN like this has several extraordinary properties which shed light on some of the properties of biological neural networks (McLeod et al., 1998):-

> **Multiple memories:** if we consider an association such as A→B or C→D to be a simple 'memory', then multiple memories can be stored on even such a simple ANN as the pattern associator described above. This contradicts the 'grandmother cell' hypothesis – the idea that a memory can be localised to a single neuron. In both biological and ANNs multiple memories can be stored on the same network.

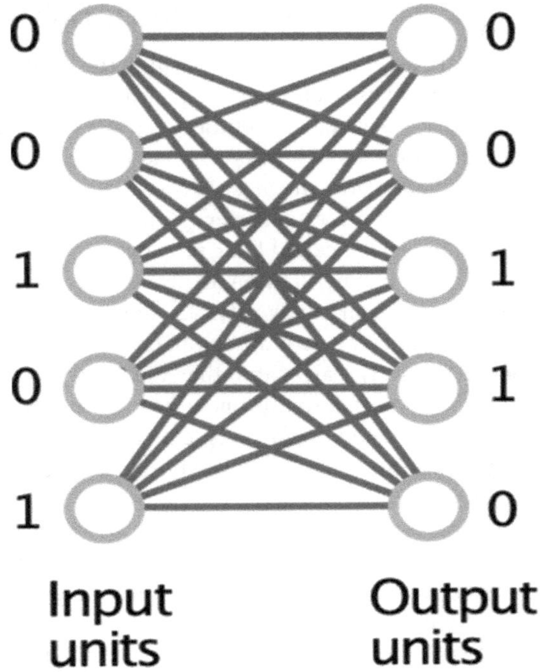

FIGURE 9.5 Layout of a simple pattern associator. Each output unit has incoming connections from every unit in the input layer, and each of these connections has an associated weight. In this example, the network is being trained to associate "00101" (code for "E") with "00110" (code for "F"). Diagram by Peter Haslehurst, adapted from McLeod et al. (1998).

Resilience to damage: even a simple two-layer pattern associator as described above is fairly resilient to damage. If, after training the network, one of the artificial neurons is deleted, the network will carry on producing more or less correct responses. If more are deleted we see a gradual degradation of performance until, at some point, it goes catastrophically downhill. This is reminiscent of what happens with neurodegenerative diseases. In the initial stages of the disease plasticity compensates for the losses and the person can carry on functioning, but at some point the deficits accelerate (Liss et al., 2021).

Pattern recognition: consider a more challenging task, which can still be taken on by a simple two-layer pattern associator – recognising a handwritten digit. During training the input layer is repeatedly fed an array of binary digits corresponding to the pixels in an image of a handwritten digit associated with a binary pattern corresponding to a number between 0 and 9 on the output layer. After training, presentation of say a handwritten '5' on the input channel will usually produce the number 5 on the output layer.

DEEP LEARNING AND BACK PROPAGATION OF ERROR

However, the recognition of handwritten digits is pushing the limits of what a simple two-layer ANN can achieve. It has been found empirically that adding extra layers produces ANNs with greatly enhanced capabilities. These extra layers between the input and output layers are known as hidden layers (see Figure 9.6). Such ANNs are usually what is referred to by the phrase *deep learning*. One issue with such networks is that a simple plasticity rule no longer works very well. A commonly used and very powerful alternative learning rule is called back propagation of error. For example, returning to the recognition of handwritten digits, let us imagine that during training, when presented with a particular handwritten '2', the network gives an incorrect output, say '3'. In back propagation of error the computer calculates an error score for each neuron in the output layer. The algorithm then allocates 'blame' for this error to all the neurons that were connected to this one – strong connections bear more of the blame so their weight is adjusted downwards, etc. This process of apportioning blame and adjusting weights accordingly is repeated backwards through each hidden layer in turn (McLeod et al., 1998).

Back propagation of error is very different from what we know of most biological neural networks, where information generally flows in one direction, forwards from the neuron along the axon to the synapse. This is where the deep learning ANNs used in many AI applications begin to depart from the biological neural networks that inspired their creation. As we approach the task of thinking ethically in a post-digital context, it is important to understand where AI systems are similar to and

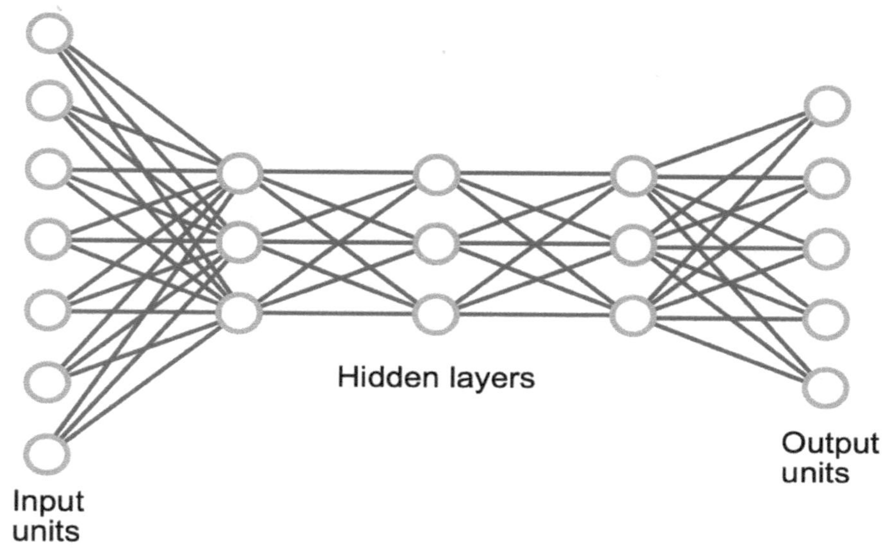

FIGURE 9.6 A simple example of a deep learning network with several hidden layers between the input and output layers. Diagram by Peter Haslehurst, adapted from McLeod et al. (1998).

where they differ from the human brain. A fruitful postdigital ethics must be able to accommodate both.

IMPLICATIONS

In this chapter, we have briefly described synaptic transmission in the human brain – the mechanism by which neurons pass information to each other. Synaptic transmission is probabilistic and, for this reason, it is misleading to think of the brain as a biological computer executing algorithms. ANNs, which are an increasingly important element in the postdigital landscape are inspired by a few very simple features of biological neural networks, such as integration, transmission strength, layers, and plasticity. Of these, plasticity is a particularly important feature, which, when applied in ANNs, has produced systems with striking capabilities such as multiple memories, resilience to damage, and pattern recognition. With more complex architectures deep learning networks have diverse and increasingly powerful capabilities, but use learning rules which are becoming increasingly divorced from the biological relevance of their forbears.

In a postdigital world it is nearly impossible to live without encountering systems which depend on digital processing and communications. Increasingly, some degree of AI is embedded in everyday systems, digital assistants, chatbots and other interfaces which encourage an anthropomorphic response from humans. We think it is important for us to recognise that digital systems, however useful, complex and intelligent do not have consciousness in the same way as humans. Thus in terms of postdigital ethics it is necessary to distinguish the various actors. Relations with an embodied intelligence (humans and other animals) are different from those with AI and other machine-based systems.

Stuart Russell, Professor of Computer Science at the University of California, Berkeley, reinforces the point about cognition that Peter makes above. Russell (2020, pp. 16–17) suggests that despite what we know about neurons and synapses, little is known about how that relates to knowing, reasoning, planning and deciding, and even less about consciousness. In his view consciousness is not relevant to how AI works, but *behaviour*: How well and consistently the set objectives are realised. This means that as machines become better and more powerful at achieving their objectives it becomes increasingly important who sets the objectives and how they are couched. AI needs to be 'not just *intelligent* but *beneficial* to humans' (Russell, 2020, pp. 9–12).

To accommodate the multifaceted dynamics of the postdigital Savin-Baden and Reader (2022, pp. xii–xiii) argue for theologies to change in the light of the challenge:

> Humans are always already grounded, embodied, implicated and entangled. Things can be alive, just as humans can be machines. So it is in specific assemblages that one needs to identify the distributed agency that is the reality of human engagement with the technical

although from what has been argued above we advocate some qualifications to identifying animals as machines.

John Reader considered that Keller is an important voice in identifying theological resources that help in considering the challenges of the postdigital. In a wide-ranging conversation with Petar Jandrić (Keller & Jandrić, 2022) it is suggested that we think of God as *potentiality*, 'the illimitable possibilities of the universe … which we … are called to actualize'. This virtuality needs to be embodied. 'Consciousness starts only when this virtual intelligence participates in the body.' This leads them on to a discussion of the Trinity referencing the work of Jurgen Moltmann (1981).

A degree of awe seems appropriate in the light of developments since Alan Turing first conceptualised what we now know as digital computers, but we would want to acknowledge that, somehow, *God* has played a part in that shared journey: *not* simply *human* creativity, but human partnership with God (Brueggemann, 1997, pp. 413–552). In this way of thinking: the *ultimate* creator gifts creative capacity and motivation to humans. Human *creatures* have freedom as to how such gifts are exercised: for the common good, for personal aggrandisement, to gain wealth and/or power.

To take a step beyond an entirely anthropocentric view injects some humility into our reflections which has been advocated at other points in the Trinity Group's work, particularly in a paper by John and Adrian Evans (Reader & Evans, 2019): humans are shaped by technology and much less in control than we imagine; we are all embedded in relationships with both other humans and the non-human world we inhabit; no over-arching framework is adequate for the complexity and plurality of the postdigital milieu.

In this spirit we offer two possibilities which support the broad ethical values we have identified: intelligence beneficial to humans, realising (human and non-human) potential and fostering creativity. We have chosen resources which we hope will be recognisable to others in the congregation we are part of. These are not offered as alternatives but, rather, with the suggestion that they are accepted as complementary: no single, over-arching account will be adequate to meet the conditions of a postdigital context. The Bible is a primary source for theological reflection but some help with interpretation is usually necessary. As a guide we have taken the Old Testament scholar Walter Brueggemann. He identifies the 'tensions, conflicts and pluralities in interpretation' (Thiselton, 2005, p. 302), bringing a 'hermeneutic of suspicion' to bear on the power structures in the text drawing on Ricouer's work (Thiselton, 2005, p. 299).

GOD AS CREATOR

A human brain, with its 85 billion neurons, is highly evolved, of great complexity, incompletely understood and pre-exists, and is pre-supposed by, attempts at self-understanding and trying to articulate where, and how, humans fit in. Yet human brains (8 or 9 billion of them), jointly and severally, are key elements of the postdigital milieu, implicated and embedded with creation and technology. Therefore we attempt not to place humans over and against, or above, other aspects of creation, including technology, in any kind of hierarchy.

The Bible begins with God as *creator* in Genesis 1:1–2. Brueggemann (2002, pp. 40–43), like Keller (Keller & Jandrić, 2022, p. 25), reminds us that creation is not out of nothing, *ex nihilo*, but out of chaos and disorder. For Brueggemann this chaos is 'an active agency … challenging the rule of YHWH … seeking to negate the prospect for well-being in the world' (Brueggemann, 2002, p. 25). Further it may be seen in the biblical accounts that humans are involved in and part of this creation alongside all the other parts of its richness and diversity.

The primary claim that God is ultimate creator and the dualism proposed between chaos and well-being lead to two statements about the relationship between God and creation in all its diversity (Brueggemann, 1997, p. 555):

God's blessing and generosity are given within a framework of accountability;

and are mitigated by chaos and disorder when 'human agents' fail in their responsibilities towards *all* creation. Where God's initiative is recognised the human response includes obligations: costs, obedience and trust, as well hope and reassurance (Brueggemann, 1997, p. 449).

God's promise of generous fruitfulness is guaranteed for *all* creatures (Brueggemann, 1997, pp. 528–531). Trust in this promise is often mitigated or absent in experience when chaos and disorder break out to nullify the blessedness. This supports an argument that creation is fragile and in jeopardy (Brueggemann, 1997, pp. 534–535). An alternative account in which God *allows* the chaos and disorder (Brueggemann, 1997, pp. 534–543) is not pursued here. 'At the root of reality (for us at least) is a *limitless generosity* that intends an extravagant abundance' (Brueggemann, 1997, p. 559).

GOD AS TRINITY

We are keen to avoid the idea that God and humans are *actors* and the rest of creation a *stage* on which the drama takes place. Reality, here, is what humans commonly inhabit and experience, in the present. Moltmann's theology grew from experiences of hope and suffering in the Second World War as well as from other theologians and philosophers including Marxist and Jewish influences (Baukham, 2005, pp. 147–148). In it 'the mutual involvement of God and the world is increasingly stressed … in which [God] both affects and is affected by the world … as a community of divine Persons who include the world within their love' (Baukham, 2005, p. 149). In his later work 'the mutual relationships of the three Persons as a perichoretic, social Trinity are the context for understanding the reciprocal relationships of God and the world' (Baukham, 2005, p. 149).

God as Trinity is implicit and not explicit in the biblical narrative appearing as distinct persons at different points. For example God's spirit 'is a decisive agency in creation' (Brueggemann, 2002, p. 200). In the New Testament Jesus gradually becomes known as 'Lord'. The doctrine achieved normative status several centuries later in the councils of the Church. Subsequently interrelations *within* God have been variously contested.

In his autobiography Moltmann (2007, pp. 287–289) writes about this new phase of work as thinking about relationships rather than power, community rather than individuals. By exploring the *sociality* in God he was 'thinking in relationships, in communities, and in transitions' instead of dividing and isolating according to what he saw to be the historic Western method. This represented a change from his earlier, dialectical thinking. Instead 'individual and community are equally primal … individual things can only be understood appropriately in their transitions in time to other states'.

The key word is *perichoresis* by which Moltmann means 'reciprocal indwelling and mutual interpenetration'. These relations are not exclusive but 'open, inviting, and embracing'.

For Bauckham, perichoresis, by involving the world, is 'trinitarian and eschatological panentheism' which allows 'freedom and equality' rather than enabling 'domination and subjection' (Baukham, 2005, p. 156). If we follow these ideas the myriad 'assemblages' and 'entanglements' of the postdigital are drawn into the dynamic activity of God on equal terms and no reality is outside God's ambit.

Including God in postdigital reality in this way suggests the possibility of 'dynamic relationality' between God, humans, digital technologies and the rest of creation where there is *no* hierarchy, 'no subordination, only mutual love in freedom'; each is *subject* to the other (Baukham, 2005, pp. 155–156). To an extent technologies function in a way *analogous* to God's spirit, mediating, but not limited to a mediating rôle. God and creation are each affected, and affect the other, are influenced by and influence the other, are enmeshed and interdependent in ways that cannot be unravelled. Humans, creation (including digital technologies) and God have degrees of freedom to act but, equally, each is constrained at points by the others.

A SUGGESTION FOR FUTURE EXPLORATION

ANNs (and the systems of which they are a part, in the widest sense of a system) are complex, beautiful and useful: they have enormous potential to enable flourishing (human and non-human), including *human* well-being and creativity. We have been deprived of the opportunity to discuss this work with John but hope that it reflects something of his openness and inclusivity to the world and to people.

CONCLUSION

It would seem reasonable to have included some consideration of the downsides while exploring possible interrelationships among God, ethical concerns, humans and digital technology in the postdigital milieu. We are concerned about the power and influence of the *Manificent Seven* alluded to in the introduction but, while beyond our present scope, some future lines of enquiry could be followed in this regard. In terms of postdigital ethics we have endorsed approaches which are negotiated, relational and share power among the agents rather than being imposed, top down or rules based. We might continue by following Keller's reminder that Biblical prophecy is 'a radical critique of systemic injustice' (Keller & Jandrić, 2022, p. 23), challenging hegemonies, often from positions of relative weakness or insignificance.

REFERENCES

Baukham, R. (2005). Jürgen Moltmann. In D. Ford & R. Muers (Eds.), *The modern theologians* (pp. 147–162). Oxford: Blackwell Publishing.

Bostrom, N. (2014). *Superintelligence: Paths, dangers, strategies.* Oxford: Oxford University Press.

Branco, T., & Staras, K. (2009). The probability of neurotransmitter release: Variability and feedback control at single synapses. *Nature Reviews Neuroscience, 10*(5), 373–383. https://doi.org/10.1038/nrn2634

Brueggemann, W. (1997). *Theology of the old testament.* Minneapolis, MN: Fortress Press.

Brueggemann, W. (2002). *Reverberations of faith.* Louisville, KY: Westminster John Knox Press.

Jandrić, P., Knox, J., Besley, T., Ryberg, T., Suoranta, J., & Hayes, S. (2018). Postdigital science and education. *Educational Philosophy and Theory, 50*(10), 893–899. https://doi.org/10.1080/00131857.2018.1454000

Kandel, E. R., Koester, J., Mack, S. H., & Siegelbaum, S. (Eds.). (2021). *Principles of neural science* (6th ed.). New York: McGraw-Hill.

Keller, C., & Jandrić, P. (2022). Process theology against global capitalism: Towards an ecological civilization. In M. Savin-Baden & J. Reader (Eds.), *Postdigital theologies: Technology, belief, and practice* (pp. 21–37). Cham: Springer.

Liss, J. L., Seleri Assunção, S., Cummings, J., Atri, A., Geldmacher, D. S., Candela, S. F., Devanand, D. P., Fillit, H. M., Susman, J., Mintzer, J., Bittner, T., Brunton, S. A., Kerwin, D. R., Jackson, W. C., Small, G. W., Grossberg, G. T., Clevenger, C. K., Cotter, V., Stefanacci, R., … Sabbagh, M. N. (2021). Practical recommendations for timely, accurate diagnosis of symptomatic Alzheimer's disease (MCI and dementia) in primary care: A review and synthesis. *Journal of Internal Medicine, 290*(2), 310–334. https://doi.org/10.1111/joim.13244

Matsuzaki, M., Honkura, N., Ellis-Davies, G. C. R., & Kasai, H. (2004). Structural basis of long-term potentiation in single dendritic spines. *Nature, 429*(6993), 761–766. https://doi.org/10.1038/nature02617

McLeod, P., Plunkett, K., & Rolls, E. T. (1998). *Introduction to connectionist modelling of cognitive processes.* Oxford: Oxford University Press.

Moltmann, J. (1981). *The trinity and the kingdom of God.* London: SCM Press.

Moltmann, J. (2007). *A broad place.* London: SCM Press.

Reader, J., & Evans, A. (2019). *Ethics after new materialism: A modest undertaking.* Rochdale, UK: William Temple Foundation.

Rennison, J. (2024). 'Magnificent seven.' *The New York Times.*

Russell, S. (2020). *Human compatible.* London: Penguin Books.

Savin-Baden, M., & Reader, J. (Eds.). (2022). *Postdigital theologies: Technology, belief, and practice.* Cham: Springer.

Thiselton, A. (2005). Biblical interpretation. In D. Ford & R. Muers (Eds.), *The modern theologians* (pp. 287–304). Oxford: Blackwell Publishing.

Part IV

Endings

10 Enfolding or Unfolding the Face

A Digital Spirituality

John Reader

> The human face carries mystery and is the exposure point of the mystery of the individual life. It is where the private, inner world of a person protrudes into the anonymous world. While the rest of the body is covered, the face is naked.
>
> *(O'Donohue, 1999)*

> the aim of algorithmic face recognition is not simply to link a given face to a private individual but rather to use facial images as a source of pre-personal and supra-personal information. At the pre-personal level, algorithmic face recognition fragments the face into bits of information that no longer belong to a private individual, but rather constitute a data bank of face templates and training sets.
>
> *(Bueno, 2020)*

What are the prospects then of the face being a mirror of the soul and a pathway into spirituality, when the technology of algorithmic facial recognition is being increasingly deployed in a range of different contexts? Exploring the subject before encountering the dangers of facial recognition and from a more philosophical as well as pastoral perspective, I suggested the following: Malabou (2016) argues that Kant suggests that the imagination plays the role of a middle term between the understanding and intuition (p. 114). It produces 'the pure look' that makes any objective encounter possible a priori. Thinking and objectivity agree with each other from the start. Imagination opens the horizon prior to the encounter so it becomes a matter of understanding that time itself is at stake in this discussion. In other words, there are what I called in 'Blurred Encounters' a pre-autonomous moment or encounter which precedes what then develops into a deeper relationship or analysis of a particular situation (Reader, 2005, p. 102). Human connection can only begin once that encounter has taken place, and that is something which is neither planned nor controlled – the very first glance or moment of eye contact between two people which then sparks off a relationship, for instance.

Derrida, whose work can also figure in this, talks about reason as 'acquiescing to the testimony of the other' and also as hospitality, both of which suggest that there has to be a willingness and openness to receive the other as they are before any further encounter can take place or develop (1999). Is it the case that digital technology

DOI: 10.1201/9781003497950-14

now pre-empts that moment of encounter, or the exercise of the imagination as Kant and Malabou would describe it? To put this in its simplest terms, digital technology operates on the basis of logic, so instead of imagination playing the role of mediating or presenting that initial moment or look, this is now going to be communicated via a system where a more means-end instrumental process is in play. Does this mean that the more human dimension which relies upon our individual capacity to perceive, interpret and then respond is no longer part of the equation?

Stiegler (2016) argues that the speed at which digital technology functions can pre-empt the process of critical thought and questioning, so this would be an equivalent concern when it comes to those initial pre-autonomous encounters. Is the very action of hospitality, welcoming or being open to the other itself now determined by a more mechanical or logic-driven process?

We know, for instance, that the use of algorithms in marketing presents us with predictions about our wants and desires based on past actions. The future comes at us in the present based on calculations of what we have done in the past, and this might indeed pre-empt any effort we would be inclined to make to consider different options. Time itself is being reconfigured by these mechanisms. If there can be such a thing as the spirituality of the digital encountering the other through the face and the unfolding of this encounter through time would appear to be vital to this understanding. It would also seem that facial recognition technology represents an enfolding or enclosure of the other for purposes of marketing or security. This demands further exploration.

I will begin with a more detailed exposition of the two extracts at the beginning of the chapter.

The quote from *Anam Cara* comes from a chapter headed 'The Face is the Icon of Creation' (p. 61). The author is attempting to hold the tension between the supposed universality of the human face and its entry into the individual person together. The face as the icon of creation is where the universe first becomes resonant with itself. 'The face is the mirror of the mind' (p. 62). The breadth of presence in the face overflows the physical form as each face is a particular intensity of human presence. Meeting again an old friend face to face is a joy all of its own because of this intensity. 'The face always reveals the soul' (p. 63). Looking at someone else's face, one gazes deeply into their life, is the claim here. This immediately raises the question of whether or not, or the extent to which this can be the case when the encounter is on a screen and mediated by digital technology. Can there still be that level of intensity which comes from those moments of eye contact? There can be real connection as has been discovered as a result of the pandemic and encounters on Zoom or the equivalent, both in terms of existing relationships and new ones. That intensity which goes beyond mere connection into realms of intimacy and deeper encounter? I think I would argue not.

Yet is this to expect too much of the encounter which comes with physical presence and to escape into the sphere of the romantic? O'Donohue continues: 'The human person is a threshold where many infinities meet' (p. 65). So, a world lies hidden beneath each human face: vulnerability, turbulence, a primal inner presence even. The gaze goes beyond the individual and into something deeper and eternal, where the mystery of our own existence stares back at us. 'Heidegger said, very beautifully, that we are custodians of deep and ancient thresholds. In the human face you see that potential and the miracle of undying possibility' (p. 67).

Levinas makes a similar claim:'

> … when I speak of the face of the other, the trace of Infinity, or the Word of God, is that of a signifying of meaning that, originally, is not a theme, is not an object of any field of knowledge, is not the being of a being, is not representation'.
>
> *(Levinas, 1999, p. 169)*

The face of the neighbour imposes on me a gratuitous and non-transferable responsibility and raises the question of justice, according to Levinas. The self is put into question by this encounter with the other, not on the basis of a common space but across the divide which is between us, so the face opposes violence by a form of metaphysical resistance. This feels like an encounter which cannot be mediated by the digital but requires that awareness of a threshold being breeched. Is this to claim too much and to place too much emphasis upon a physical presence?

One notes that there is a real debate here between those of us who are concerned with what I have called disincarnation and the detachment of the human from that physical presence which can have serious political and environmental consequences by encouraging an escape into the metaverse or other forms of virtual reality (Reader, 2022, 2023), and theologians such as Joshua K. Smith. In Robot Theology (2022) Smith suggests that there is room in the Christian metaphysic and ecclesiology for a qualified disembodied presence (p. 122). While this might not be normative, it should be allowed and supported. 'God, Jesus and the Holy Spirit are invisible persons. Embracing strict theological physicalism seems to conflict with the biblical reality that presence is not merely about biological material or embodiment' (p. 123). Since disembodied presence as mediated by the digital has now become a reality in church life, Smith is right that there is a real issue here of how this is to be interpreted. Virtual and augmented reality are still reality and also still material, but are there limits of what can be encountered through them and what might this mean for spirituality? When apps, Instagram and other forms of social media are being used for religious purposes, how can one square this with the dangers of distortions threatened through facial recognition technology?

WHAT CAN WE LEARN FROM THE CRITIQUES OF FACIAL RECOGNITION TECHNOLOGY?

Bueno's article is important in that it both sets out the actual technologies and also engages with the political and philosophical dimensions of current practices. Facial recognition relies on machine-learning algorithms which can be trained to define their own rules for face identification and face analysis. An algorithm is provided with a large dataset of images of faces and after having thousands or even millions of such images fed into it can then define its own rules in a manner that may remain inaccessible to a human programmer. A 2018 algorithm based on deep neural networks has allegedly reached an accuracy of 99.5% (P75). An immediate concern has been racial bias in these processes where the datasets have been largely of white subjects.

Bueno raises the issue of how Christianity encouraged the idea of a 'universal face'. So Christ appears both as a sign of his individuality and as a sign of universal humanity. (O'Donohue has shades of this as we have seen.) The problem is that once this has become enshrined in a capitalist political culture of control and enclosure it is too readily translated into a reductionist interpretation in which individuality is subsumed beneath the datasets which function at scale. It is no longer the individual who is of interest to police and security forces, for instance, but the wider population as subjects of interest on a statistical basis. Deleuze (1995, p. 180) has suggested that there has been a shift to a control regime of power where information technologies are being used to replace the mass/individual dyad with 'dividuals' and 'data banks'. The digital self becomes a cog in a larger machine of big data and statistical predictability. It is the behaviour of given groups or populations which is the subject of such predictions rather than that of specific individuals. It is no longer about identity then.

In other words there are two different but related processes now taking place according to Bueno. He uses Deleuze and Guattari's definitions of social subjection and machinic enslavement (p. 81).

> In machinic enslavement, therefore, there are no subjects, just bodies, affects and flows of energy that modulate a larger unity. In social subjection, on the contrary, subjects are produced as the higher unity which relates externally to other objects .... Whereas in machinic enslavement humans are 'enslaved by the machine', in social subjection they are subjected to it.
>
> *(p. 82)*

We either have subjects or dividuals, but in neither case could these be the individuals who would be persons who encounter others, or the others who are encountered as understood within traditional spirituality. There are either fragmented flows of data or huge aggregates. It is easy then to see how bias and forms of injustice readily creep into these processes and the face becomes a locus of external control.

This is a deeply pessimistic interpretation of current deployments of facial recognition technology, and neither Bueno nor Deleuze and Guattari offer any real practical examples of how these enclosures and enfoldings might be challenged or disrupted by the thresholds or unfoldings that a Christian spirituality would be seeking. Bueno even disputes whether political struggles for data protection and privacy have any real impact as they focus only on the domain of social subjection and neglect the machinic dimension of algorithmic face recognition (p. 88). Other than a 'dismantling of the face' or a deeper engagement with Deleuze's understandings of the reflective or the intensive face, the alternatives seem to have run into the ground.

On 28 March 2023, the BBC ran the following disturbing story. Facial recognition firm Clearview has run nearly a million searches for US police, its founder has told the BBC. CEO Hoan Ton-That also revealed Clearview now has 30 billion images scraped from platforms such as Facebook, taken without users' permissions. The company has been repeatedly fined millions of dollars in Europe and Australia for breaches of privacy. Critics argue that the police's use of Clearview puts everyone into a 'perpetual police line-up'.

'Whenever they have a photo of a suspect, they will compare it to your face', says Matthew Guaragilia from the Electronic Frontier Foundation says. 'It's far too invasive.' Clearview's system allows a law enforcement customer to upload a photo of a face and find matches in a database of billions of images it has collected. It then provides links to where matching images appear online. It is considered one of the most powerful and accurate facial recognition companies in the world.

As if this is not worrying enough, the next stage of the development of the technology which is already well underway is the aim of being able to identify emotions. If emotions, then what about whatever we might mean by spirituality? In her book *Atlas of* AI (2021), Kate Crawford recounts the narrative behind these developments (Chapter 5). It began back in 1967 with the work of a young American psychologist, Paul Ekman, and his research in Papua New Guinea. 'He was gathering evidence to bolster a controversial hypothesis: that all humans exhibit a small number of universal emotions or affect that are natural, innate, cross-cultural, and the same all over the world' (p. 151). Even though this claim is heavily disputed and the evidence questionable, it has triggered an industry that is now worth over 17 billion dollars. So begins the story of what Crawford calls, affect recognition, and how this is now part of AI technology and its use.

How then is the technology likely to be deployed? Police forces, the military, intelligence agencies and corporations each have a stake, holding out the prospect of being able to distinguish friend from foe, lies from truth, and being able to penetrate into our inner worlds. Facial recognition claims to be able to identify a particular individual – although as Beuno argues this is perhaps more to do with the collective than is realised – but affect recognition aims to detect and classify emotions by analysing any face. AI giants such as Amazon, Microsoft and IBM have all designed systems intended to function in this way (p. 195). They work on similar assumptions; that there is a small number of distinct and universal emotional categories that we involuntarily reveal in our faces and that these can be detected by machines.

Ekman's research is far from universally accepted but this does not seem to have had any bearing on further research and potential deployment. The idea that there are universal facial traits across different cultures, let alone that they can be correctly identified by the technologies are both disputed. Ekman has sold techniques of deception detection to security agencies which then use them in screening programmes such as those put into operation after 9/11. This system uses a set of 94 criteria, all alleged signs of stress, fear or deception. This means that some groups are automatically disadvantaged, as anyone who is under stress during questioning (and who would not be?) scores higher. This produces its own form of racial profiling and potential discrimination.

The cultural anthropologist Margaret Mead is unconvinced by Ekman's claim that there are universal, biological determinants of behaviour as this discounts cultural factors. Whereas Ekman sets up a binary according to which emotions are either universal or they are not, her approach is more nuanced, arguing that cultural factors can play a part even though there may be a core of innate human behaviours (p. 171). One of the most important critics of this whole approach though is the psychologist Lisa Feldman Barrett (2017). She challenges any form of essentialism when it comes to the emotions, based on the evidence of neuroscience disputing both the classical view that there is a danger of relativism and the constructivist interpretation that all is relative and culturally determined. We are neither blank slates nor are we putty to be shaped purely by external influences.

> When we peer into the workings of a functioning brain, we don't see mental modules. We see core systems that interact continuously in complex ways to produce many sorts of minds, depending on culture. The human brain is itself a cultural artifact because it is wired by experience. We have genes that are turned on and off by the environment, and other genes that regulate how sensitive to the environment we are.... I am perhaps the first one to point out how brain evolution, brain development, and its resulting anatomy point in a clear direction for the science of emotion and our view of human nature.
>
> *(Barrett, p. 170)*

In other words, neither biological determinism nor cultural determinism are correct. What does this mean for the claims to be able to detect emotions by facial recognition? Barrett is clear that despite all the research and investment of the technology companies, some of the most pressing questions about emotion remain unanswered and important questions remain obscured because many businesses and scientists continue to practice essentialism while the rest are still trying to figure out how emotions are made. 'The facts remain that no one has found even a single reliable, broadly replicable, objectively measurable essence of emotion' (p. 173).

As Crawford goes on to say drawing on Barrett's research, facial expressions are far from indisputable and are not fingerprints or diagnostic displays that reliably signal emotional states, either across cultures or across contexts. In which case the whole project to read emotions through facial recognition technology is deeply flawed. Yet the investment continues and even more worryingly as we see with that account of Clearview, is operationalised on a large scale in ways that are likely to be discriminatory and authoritarian. So what are the alternatives?

DELEUZE (AND GUATTARI) ON THE FACE

Having reviewed the political implications of what one can draw from Deleuze's work on the subject it is worth returning to some of his more substantive writing on the subject, plus his collaboration with Guattari. In 'Cinema 1' (2013) in the course of his lengthy exposition of what he calls the Affection Image (Chapter 6) he outlines what he sees as the normal purposes of the facial image. This is in the context of close-ups used in cinema graphics. Ordinarily, three roles of the face are recognisable: it is individuating (it distinguishes or characterizes each person); it is socialising (it manifests a social role); it is relational or communicating (it ensures not only communication between two people, but also in a single person, the internal agreement between his character and his role) (p. 110). He goes on to say that in the case of a close-up, all three of these aspects are lost. This may be difficult to understand at first, but he is arguing that there is no close-up of the face but rather that the close-up is the face itself insofar as those three functions have been destroyed. The principle of individuation ceases to hold sway, as do the other two functions. 'The close-up does not divide one individual any more than it reunites two: it suspends individuation' (p. 111). Referring to the work of Bergman in particular, Deleuze says 'the facial close-up is both the face and its effacement' (p. 111). If one then transposes this to the sphere of facial recognition, one might present a similar argument.

What is happening here is not about establishing the identity of a person as an individual, but about their existence as a possible threat or as an entity available for marketing purposes. The face has been effaced. Similarly, they are not of interest because of their social role, nor indeed because of their capacity to relate to or communicate with others. That being the case, those normal functions of the face are replaced by what are configurations of power and potential external control. Even worse perhaps from the point of view of any form of spirituality, any connection between their internal character and external appearance is either lost or subsumed by these security or marketing considerations. The face is reduced to a set of data or measurable components. Another close-up in which the face as mirror of the soul or any form of individual identity is effaced.

What Deleuze seems to be saying is that there is a dimension of an interpretation of the facial that is in danger of being lost through the deployment of any technology which deals with faces as simply images. In an earlier stage of this argument, he refers to the work of Peirce who distinguishes between what he terms a 'Firstness' and a 'Secondness' (p. 109). There is a difference between the affect or entity and that which expresses it: 'the affect does not exist independently of something which expresses it, although it is completely distinct from it' (p. 108). What expresses it is a face or a facial equivalent. One can call the set of the expressed and its expression, of the affect and of the face, 'icon'. The icon has a different form and a different function and there are icons of feature and icons of outline. This is the sign of what Deleuze calls the affection-image. The affection-image has a power and quality of its own being the expressions which are embodied in states of things. This, however, becomes abstracted into action-images once this is actualised through emotion, impulse or sensation.

This latter would seem to be what Peirce means by 'Secondness', where one encounters forces or actualisations in specific states of things be those determinate space-times, geographical milieux, collective agents or individual people. Where the actual becomes real there is 'Secondness' as something new and different emerges which is to be distinguished from 'Firstness'. Deleuze suggests that Peirce finds this Firstness difficult to define because it is felt rather than perceived: 'it concerns what is new in experience, what is fresh, fleeting and nevertheless eternal' (p. 109). Rather than being a sensation in itself or an idea or feeling, it is the quality of a possible sensation or feeling. As such Firstness is the category of the Possible and expresses the possible without actualising it, while making it a complete mode.

However difficult this is to understand, one might speculate whether both Deleuze and Peirce are struggling to articulate that which might be behind the idea that the face is a mirror of the soul. In other words, behind any particular external expression or actualisation available through the image of the face, there lies something deeper and impenetrable that Deleuze calls the Possible, that which is fresh and nevertheless eternal. In which case one can question whether any presentation of the face as image, whether close-up or subject of datafication for external purposes of control, can ever be true to that other level or dimension. Is the use of facial recognition technology so alien to that dimension which we might refer to as the spiritual, that the only outcome can be distortion and betrayal? As the face is effaced so indeed is the soul.

ALTERNATIVE FACES

The account of Deleuze provided so far is not the end of the story however, at least, not as interpreted by Moore (2023). Referring again to 'Cinema 1', Moore points out that Deleuze presents us with two possibilities for the face, the reflective face and the intensive face (p. 214). Linking these to the face of Christ, Moore suggests that the reflective version reveals a 'lowborn Jewish peasant become All-Sovereign Ruler and Judge' (p. 215). Whereas 'the intensive face is a would-be escaping face, intent on pursuing a line of flight from the faciality machine itself' (p. 215). In other words, we encounter a Janus-faced Jesus split down the middle, affectively vibrant on one side and a divine imperial judge on the other. The latter is a dark side in that it presents a God become (white) man whose followers will weaponise his whiteness to oppress those who are different. So, does the intensive face hold out the hope of a real alternative and what might this look like?

Moving on to examine Deleuze and Guattari together in 'A Thousand Plateaus' (2008), Moore argues that they present Jesus once again as a standard face, so white and still in thrall to the ambitions of imperialist powers. There can be deviances to this, but little real evidence of serious alternatives operating within a faith context. 'In place of a single line of partition between an absolute Inside and an absolute Outside, Deleuze and Guattari posit multiple dividing lines, multiple gradations of divergence and deviance' (p. 218). Yet the dominant face is still the white one and alternatives are hard to identify and sustain against this background.

There is a degree of hope in their philosophy though, according to Moore, if one relates their ideas to the account of the Road to Emmaus in St Luke's Gospel. The Jesus who approaches the two disciples on the road is unrecognisable, a disincarnated face floating free of a body, until the point where he breaks bread with them, shares it and then disappears. The disciples then head back to Jerusalem to recount their experience. Moore interprets this as

> what the disciples have constructed … from their encounter with the mysterious but mundane figure on the road is a foreign-born migrant who is entirely incognizant of local conditions, but whose presence, as such, is a provocation, an invitation, to radical hospitality.
>
> *(p. 225)*

The disciples extend their invitation to him to 'stay with us', and one could argue that as the head of the stranger begins to appear as ever less white, then this extends the process to migrants, refugees, asylum seekers and all those apparently outside the traditional normality represented by the white Jesus. Reflecting on the implications of this for the wider question of race. Moore suggests that

> nonbinary proliferation is the answer implicit in the question, virtual profusions, an open-ended multiplication of the potentialities for being racially embodied, and racially embedded, in the world. For race is not always, or not only, a mechanism of containment, an implement of oppression.
>
> *(p. 230)*

In which case here are real alternatives, thresholds which challenge the enclosures created by facial images and the digital technology which operates through them. An unfolding which disrupts the enfolding characteristic of reducing faces to data and images to mechanisms of control. Linking this to biblical accounts as Moore does offers a hope of connecting to spirituality as a site of resistance. Hospitality appears once again as central to this as it has done before in the works of Derrida and Levinas. Being open and welcoming to the other breaks open the shackles of prejudice embedded in the technologies as one encounters the mirrors in their faces.

FOLDS OF THE SOUL

Deleuze is even more explicit on this subject in 'The Fold' (2010), and reference to this will set up the final stage of this exploration. He says:

> Folds are in the soul and authentically exist only in the soul. That is already true for 'innate ideas': they are pure Virtualities, pure powers whose act consists in habitus or arrangements (folds) in the soul, and whose completed act consists of an inner action of the soul (an internal deployment)
>
> *(p. 24)*

This is of course Deleuze's own interpretation of Leibniz but it does cohere with the ideas described earlier. He continues that the soul is not in a body, in a point, but is itself a higher point and of another nature. Rather than being identified with the Platonic idea of the One, this refers to a multiplicity which is inseparable from the folds that are made when the One is enveloped, and of unfoldings when it is developed. Here we have movement, intensity and immanence, complicating and entangling, rather than hierarchy and transcendence. The best way of describing this process is as unfolding and thus releasing through thresholds the multiple possibilities talked about in the context of the face and faciality. This theme is picked and taken further by Latour in 'An Inquiry Into Modes of Existence' Chapter 8 (2013).

Latour asks how the Moderns have managed to miss the strangeness, the ubiquity, and yes, the spirituality of technology (p. 210). He argues that the adjective 'technological' does not designate in the first place an object, a result, but a movement that is going to take from inert entities and from living ones what is needed to hold together in a lasting way, to freeze, as it were, one of the moments of metamorphosis. What is lasting and persistent in these things depends on the presence of composites that have been drawn out by metamorphoses from the persistence of beings of reproduction, each of which lends certain of its virtues, but most often without leaving us the possibility of profiting from its initiative and its autonomy in a lasting way. The ingredients of these blends always remain foreign to one another. They 'lend themselves as the expression puts it so well, to being translated, deflected, disposed, arranged, but they nevertheless remain 'themselves' ready to go at the slightest pretext' (walls fall down wood is eaten away, etc.) (p. 225).

To say that technologies are effective, transparent, or mastered is to take the conclusion for the pathways that lead to them. It is to miss their spirit, their genesis, their beauty, their truth. Latour asks what is the equivalent for the zigzags, the brilliant flashes, the detours and discontinuities, of *chains of reference* for objective knowledge, *processions* for religion, *means* for the passage of law, *persistence* for the beings of reproduction. We shall call it technical FOLDING (p. 227). The term 'folding' will allow us to avoid the blunder of speaking of technology irreverently as a piling up of objects or as an admirable example of mastery, transparence, rationality, that would prove 'man's dominion over matter'. Technology always entails folds upon folds, implications, complications and explanations. Its canonical representation, thoroughly studied by the sociology of technologies, sketches it in the form of a series, often a very long series, of nested TRANSLATIONS, a labyrinth. Once we have been freed of our obsession with matter, nothing prevents us from identifying the diversity of these differentials. What counts each time, is not the type of material but the difference in the relative resistance of what is bound together. Curiously, Latour argues, there is nothing material in technology. Where there is differential resistance and heterogeneity among the components, technology is found as well.

CONCLUSION

Given Latour's exposition of what elements might be relevant to a spirituality of technology, what else could be added to these by our examination of the practical example of facial recognition technologies? First, the technologies need to become sites of resistance as and when they are used as mechanisms of dominance or control. Second, they need to be ways of opening up to others as different and multiple through the exercise of hospitality as found within the Christian tradition. They become those alternative spaces as they unfold rather than being enfolded or mechanisms of enclosure as seems so often the case under the dominance of Big Tech companies. Third, this requires the exercise of the imagination in such a way as to challenge or bypass the overly mathematical or logical operations of the technologies and their tendency to contract the times for reflection rather than enhancing them. One might suggest that there is such a thing as 'the Spiritual Commons' which requires protecting and nourishing in order that those other dimensions of the human can flourish in relation to that which lies beyond. Technology entails folds upon folds so engagement with the spiritual demands attention to the nature of those folds and the will to open them up rather than to close them down for the purposes of external control. The face can still be a mirror of the soul.

REFERENCES

Barrett, L.F. (2017). *How Emotions Are Made: The Secret Life of the Brain.* London, UK: Pan Books.

Bueno, C.C. (2020). The Face Revisited: Using Deleuze and Guattari to Explore the Politics of Algorithmic Face Recognition. *Theory, Culture and Society*, Vol. 37(1). 73–91.

Crawford, K. (2021). *Atlas of AI.* New Haven, CT and London: Yale University Press.

Deleuze, G. (1995). *Negotiations 1972–1990.* New York: Columbia University Press.

Deleuze, G. (2010). *The Fold.* London, UK: Continuum.

Deleuze, G. (2013). *Cinema 1: The Movement Image.* London, UK: Bloomsbury Academic Press.

Deleuze, G. and Guattari, F. (2008). *A Thousand Plateaus.* London, UK: Continuum.

Derrida, J. (1999). *Adieu: To Emmanuel Levinas.* Stanford, CA: Stanford University Press.
Latour, B. (2013). *An Inquiry into Modes of Existence: An Anthropology of the Moderns.* Harvard, MA: Harvard University Press.
Levinas, E. (1999). *Alterity and Transcendence.* London, UK: The Athlone Press.
Malabou, C. (2016). *Before Tomorrow: Epigenesis and Rationality.* Cambridge, UK: Polity Press.
Moore, S.D. (2023). *The Bible after Deleuze: Affects, Assemblages, Bodies without Organs.* Oxford, UK: Oxford University Press.
O'Donohue, J. (1999). *Anam Cara: Spiritual Wisdom from the Celtic World.* London, UK: Bantam Books.
Reader, J. (2005). *Blurred Encounters: A Reasoned Practice of Faith.* Vale of Glamorgan, Wales: Aureus Publishing.
Reader, J. (2022). *The Digital and the Environmental.* William Temple Foundation Ethical Futures Tract. Rochdale, UK: William Temple Foundation.
Reader, J. (2023). *Postdigital Research and Human Agency.* Chapter in Postdigital Research: Postdigital Science and Education Series. Cham: Springer.
Smith, J.K. (2022). *Robot Theology: Old Questions through New Media.* Eugene, OR: Wipf and Stock.
Stiegler, B. (2016). *Automatic Society: Volume 1: The Future of Work.* Cambridge, UK: Polity Press.

Final Reflections on the Text

Maria Power

I first met John Reader in 2014 through the William Temple Foundation where we were both Senior Research Fellows and when I moved to Oxford in 2018, he invited me to join the Trinity Group. The Trinity Group, broadly linked to the William Temple Foundation Ethical Futures Group, was an eclectic group of academics, practitioners and clergy who were all interested in the same thing: ethics or, to put it more precisely, the role of ethics in the rapidly changing world in which we live. Conversations covered a wide range of topics from whether using an Alexa (or other AI assistant) was safe to the impact of the digital on our brains to our rights to water. What began as a series of group discussions developed into a wide-ranging seminar series. In this collection of essays, you can see some of the fruits of our discussions.

What John Reader prompted in many of us was the need to care and to be more considerate about justice in a digital age. We are currently experiencing a technological revolution, which many argue has not been seen since the invention of the printing press in 1436 or beginning of the industrial revolution in the 18th century. Yet I suggest this is a much bigger revolution. Technology is changing rapidly, almost daily one could argue. This is having an impact on education, the environment and the way we pray, to name but three examples. However, the most important consequences of such rapid, and often ill thought, developments are in our relationships with one another, with society and the ethical consequences of how we use technology.

Many of the consequences that have brought good and positive outcomes: We can now speak easily to friends living on the other side of the world without having to book a phone call (as we used to have to when I was a child), migration no longer means losing touch with loved ones as we can keep in contact through the miniature computers that we carry around with us. It is easier to find a romantic partner through one of the many apps available and we can follow the life updates of people we went to school with but lost touch with in the predigital age. Shopping is easier and websites such as Project Gutenberg give us access to 1,000s of books that we would previously have only been able to access through a copyright library. So far, so good. We can shop, talk to people and read books through the wonder of technology.

Yet the negative consequences are hiding in plain sight however and are also affecting the ways we live our lives. Documents posted on the WikiLeaks website have shown how algorithms played a crucial part in Brexit and the election of Trump, with misinformation, dupery and fake news playing a key role in the results. Additionally, it is now far easier to become radicalised be it into the far right or Islamic extremism – the consequences of which can often be fatal. The digital has

DOI: 10.1201/9781003497950-15

brought a new dimension to bullying meaning that victims can be followed and tracked at all times. It is now quite common to hear of suicides resulting from online bullying and sexual harassment. Meanwhile, the world faces a climate crisis, the result of which can be seen in burning forests and increased severe weather events. I could go on.

John was prescient in his interests in the digital and the environment. He was thinking, speaking and writing about the ethical issues we would face long before most of us had mastered Facebook. He was correct in most of his concerns. This collection of essays is a testament to the influence that he had on a wide range of scholars, and I hope it will inspire us to continue the conversations that he began.

Index

Note: **Bold** page numbers refer to tables and *italic* page numbers refer to figures.

N

O

P

Q

R

S

Kolibri 360 GmbH
Ferdinand-Jühlke-Straße 7
99095 Erfurt, Deutschland
produktsicherheit@kolibri360.de